Residential Electricity Consumption in Urbanizing China

T0299850

This book forges a link between residential CO_2 emissions and time use, focussing on China as a key case study.

To provide a better understanding of the energy implications of the lifestyle differences between urban and rural China, Pui Ting Wong and Yuan Xu utilise time-use methodology as an alternative way to explore the links between individual lifestyle and residential electricity consumption. They begin by examining how Chinese citizens divide their time between daily activities, highlighting patterns around indicators including age, gender, education, and economic status. They go on to quantify CO_2 intensities of these time-use activities. Through this linkage, this book presents an alternative strategy for climate-friendly living, highlighting the ways in which urban planning can be deployed to help individuals adapt their time-use patterns for CO_2 mitigation.

Providing a novel contribution to the growing literature on residential electricity consumption, *Residential Electricity Consumption in Urbanizing China* will be of great interest to scholars of climate policy, energy studies, time use, and urban planning.

Pui Ting Wong is a Ph.D. student in the Rachel Carson Center for Environment and Society, LMU Munich, Germany.

Yuan Xu is an Associate Professor in the Department of Geography and Resource Management at the Chinese University of Hong Kong. He is also leading the Environmental Policy and Governance Programme in the Institute of Environment, Energy, and Sustainability.

Routledge Focus on Energy Studies

Limits to Terrestrial Extraction
Robert E. Kirsch

Network Governance and Energy Transitions in European Cities
Timea Nochta

Residential Electricity Consumption in Urbanizing China
Time Use and Climate-Friendly Living
Pui Ting Wong and Yuan Xu

For more information about this series, please visit: www.routledge.com/Routledge-Focus-on-Energy-Studies/book-series/RFENS

Residential Electricity Consumption in Urbanizing China

Time Use and Climate-Friendly Living

Pui Ting Wong and Yuan Xu

LONDON AND NEW YORK

from Routledge

First published 2022
by Routledge
4 Park Square, Milton Park, Abingdon, Oxon OX14 4RN

and by Routledge
605 Third Avenue, New York, NY 10158

Routledge is an imprint of the Taylor & Francis Group, an informa business

© 2022 Pui Ting Wong and Yuan Xu

British Library Cataloguing-in-Publication Data
A catalogue record for this book is available from the British Library

Library of Congress Cataloging-in-Publication Data
A catalog record has been requested for this book

ISBN: 978-0-367-26148-1 (hbk)
ISBN: 978-1-032-26846-0 (pbk)
ISBN: 978-0-429-29170-8 (ebk)

DOI: 10.4324/9780429291708

Typeset in Times
by SPi Technologies India Pvt Ltd (Straive)

Contents

List of figures   vii
List of tables   xii
Preface   xiii

1   Introduction   **1**

    1.1 Climate change and China's residential sector   1
    1.2 Lifestyle and residential energy consumption   7
        1.2.1 Residential energy consumption   7
        1.2.2 Urbanization and residential energy consumption   9
        1.2.3 Demographic change and residential energy
            consumption   12
    1.3 Time use as a residential lifestyle indicator   14
        1.3.1 Time-use survey and applications   14
        1.3.2 Time use and energy consumption   17
    1.4 Objectives and outline   21
    References   23

2   Time use in evolving China   **31**

    2.1 The Chinese time-use survey (CTUS)   31
    2.2 Time-use-defined lifestyles in China   35
    Appendix I 2008 Chinese time-use survey   57
        Time-use diary   57
        Activity classification   58
    Appendix II 2018 Chinese time-use survey   64
        Time-use diary   64
        Activity classification   66
    References   66

3 Estimating residential electricity and CO$_2$ intensity of time-use activity   **68**

3.1 *Estimating energy intensity of time use*   68
3.2 *A bottom-up approach for constructing electricity CO$_2$
    intensity*   72
    3.2.1 *Matching electric appliances with activities*   72
    3.2.2 *Electricity intensity*   75
3.3 *Data*   77
    3.3.1 *The Chinese Residential Energy Consumption Survey
       (CRECS)*   77
    3.3.2 *Mending the mismatched datasets*   82
3.4 *Changes in electricity and CO$_2$ intensity of daily activities
    between 2008 and 2018*   86
    3.4.1 *Appliance characteristics in 2008 and 2018*   86
    3.4.2 *Sharing characteristics in 2008 and 2018*   91
    3.4.3 *Reconstructed intensity of activity in
       2008 and 2018*   93
    *Appendix I Comparison of activity categorization in
       this book, 2008 and 2018 Chinese time-use survey*   101
    *Appendix II Detailed description of appliance operation
       mode*   104
References   105

4 Residential CO$_2$ emissions of lifestyles   **108**

4.1 *Reconstructing residential CO$_2$ emissions*   108
4.2 *Residential CO$_2$ emissions by activities*   109
4.3 *Discussion*   127
References   130

5 The climate impacts of lifestyles from demographic changes   **131**

5.1 *China's demographic shifts*   131
5.2 *Climate impacts of the major ongoing demographic shifts
    in China*   134
5.3 *Climate impacts of time-use patterns*   141
5.4 *Climate impacts of time-use management*   143
References   146

6 Time-use management for carbon mitigation   **147**

6.1 *Time use and residential CO$_2$ emissions*   147
6.2 *Shaping climate-friendly time-use patterns*   150
References   154

Index   **157**

Figures

1.1   CO$_2$ emissions and key milestones   2
1.2   CO$_2$ emissions per capita   2
1.3   Primary energy consumption and CO$_2$ emissions in
      China (1980–2019)   3
1.4   Fuel mix of China's primary energy consumption (1980–2019)   4
1.5   Energy consumption by sector   5
1.6   Residential energy consumption in China (1980–2019)   6
1.7   Residential electricity consumption and its shares
      in China (1980–2019)   6
2.1   Ten Chinese provinces sampled in the 2008 and
      2018 time-use surveys   32
2.2   Lifestyle in a typical weekday in 2018 by daily time use   37
2.3   Lifestyle in a typical weekend/holiday in 2018 by daily
      time use   38
2.4   Lifestyle differences and evolution between the 2008
      and 2018 time-use surveys   39
2.5   Lifestyle of a typical urban Chinese in 2018 by daily time use   40
2.6   Lifestyle of a typical rural Chinese in 2018 by daily time use   40
2.7   Urban-rural lifestyle differences and evolution
      between the 2008 and 2018 time-use surveys   41
2.8   Urban lifestyle differences and evolution between the
      2008 and 2018 time-use surveys   42
2.9   Rural lifestyle differences and evolution between the
      2008 and 2018 time-use surveys   42
2.10 Lifestyle of a typical Chinese woman in 2018 by daily
      time use   43
2.11 Lifestyle of a typical Chinese man in 2018 by daily time use   44
2.12 Gender lifestyle differences and evolution between the
      2008 and 2018 time-use surveys   44
2.13 Gender lifestyle differences and evolution on
      weekdays between the 2008 and 2018 time-use surveys   45

2.14 Gender lifestyle differences and evolution on weekdays holidays between the 2008 and 2018 time-use surveys 45

2.15 Lifestyle variations by age between the 2008 and 2018 time-use surveys 46

2.16 Lifestyle of a typical Chinese in youth age (15–24 years old) in 2018 by daily time use 47

2.17 Lifestyle of a typical Chinese in prime working age (25–54 years old) in 2018 by daily time use 48

2.18 Lifestyle of a typical Chinese senior citizen in retirement age (65–74 years old) in 2018 by daily time use 48

2.19 Lifestyle evolution (2018 vs 2008) between the two time-use surveys. 49

2.20 Lifestyle variations by education level between the 2008 and 2018 time-use surveys 50

2.21 Lifestyle of a typical Chinese with no schooling in 2018 by daily time use 51

2.22 Lifestyle of a typical Chinese with university education or above in 2018 by daily time use 51

2.23 Lifestyle evolution (2018 vs 2008) by education level between the two time-use surveys. 52

2.24 Lifestyle variations by monthly income levels between the 2008 and 2018 time-use surveys 53

2.25 Lifestyle of a typical Chinese with low income (500–1000 RMB/month/person) in 2018 by daily time use 53

2.26 Lifestyle of a typical Chinese with high income (more than 10,000 RMB/month/person) in 2018 by daily time use 54

2.27 Lifestyle evolution (2018 vs 2008) by monthly income level between the two time-use surveys 55

2.28 Share of in-residence activities in 2008 by daily time use 56

2.29 Share of time spent at respondent's residence in 2008 time-use survey by activity and day of the week 56

3.1 The 27 sampled provinces in the 2012 Chinese Residential Energy Consumption Survey 78

3.2 Changes in Chinese time-use pattern between 2008, 2012, and 2018 83

3.3 Changes of the number of seven major appliances owned per household between 2008, 2012, and 2018 84

3.4 Changes of the power rate requirements of refrigerators, freezers and air conditioners in Chinese Energy Label Standards between 2008, 2012, and 2018 85

3.5   Changes in household size, per-capita dwelling size
      and annual income in urban and rural households
      between 2008, 2012, and 2018   86
3.6   Average number of electric appliances in urban and
      rural households, by 2008 and 2018   87
3.7   Average power rate of appliances in urban and rural
      households, by 2008 and 2018   88
3.8   Average daily usage of appliances in urban and rural
      households, by 2008 and 2018   89
3.9   Average daily electricity consumption by appliance in
      urban and rural households, by 2008 and 2018   89
3.10 Average number of household members involving in
      activities matched to an appliance, by urban and rural
      residents, by 2008 and 2018   92
3.11 Average time spent on activities matched to an appli-
      ance, by urban and rural residents, by 2008 and 2018   93
3.12 Electricity intensity of activity before calibration, by
      urban and rural residents, by 2008 and 2018   94
3.13 Daily per-capita residential electricity consump-
      tion derived from our estimation and from national
      statistics, by urban and rural residents, by 2008 and 2018   96
3.14 Residential electricity intensity of activity after
      calibration, by urban and rural residents, by 2008 and 2018   96
3.15 Residential CO_2 intensity of activity after calibration,
      by urban and rural residents, by 2008 and 2018   97
4.1   Residential CO_2 emissions in 2018 by activity   109
4.2   Residential CO_2 emissions by activity and operation
      mode of appliances in 2018   110
4.3   Shares of Residential CO_2 emissions by activity and
      operation mode of appliance in 2018   110
4.4   Change of Residential CO_2 emissions from 2008 to 2018   111
4.5   Urban residential CO_2 emissions in 2018   112
4.6   Rural residential CO_2 emissions in 2018   113
4.7   Difference of Residential CO_2 emissions between
      urban and rural residents in 2008 and 2018   114
4.8   Difference of Residential CO_2 emissions between 2008
      and 2018 for urban and rural residents   114
4.9   Difference of Residential CO_2 emissions between
      weekend and weekday in 2008 and 2018   115
4.10 Difference of Residential CO_2 emissions between 2008
      and 2018 for weekday and weekend/holiday lifestyles   116

4.11 Daily residential CO_2 emissions by men in 2018   117
4.12 Daily residential CO_2 emissions by a typical Chinese
      woman in 2018   118
4.13 Gender differences of residential CO_2 emissions   118
4.14 Difference of Residential CO_2 emissions between 2008
      and 2018 for gendered lifestyles   119
4.15 Daily residential CO_2 emissions by young Chinese
      (15–24 years old)   120
4.16 Daily residential CO_2 emissions by working-age
      Chinese (25–54 years old)   120
4.17 Daily residential CO_2 emissions by old Chinese (65–74
      years old)   121
4.18 Difference of residential CO_2 emissions between indi-
      vidual age groups   121
4.19 Difference of residential CO_2 emissions between 2008
      and 2018 by age group   122
4.20 Daily residential CO_2 emissions by people with no
      schooling in 2018   123
4.21 Daily residential CO_2 emissions by people with uni-
      versity education in 2018   123
4.22 Difference of residential CO_2 emissions between
      people with different education levels   124
4.23 Change of residential CO_2 emissions from 2008 to 2018   125
4.24 Daily residential CO_2 emissions by people with an
      income between 500 and 1,000RMB/month in 2018   125
4.25 Daily residential CO_2 emissions by people with an
      income higher than 10,000RMB/month in 2018   126
4.26 Difference of residential CO_2 emissions between
      people with different income levels   126
4.27 Change of residential CO_2 emissions from 2008 to 2018   127
5.1   Urban, rural population and urbanization rate in China   132
5.2   Age composition and elderly dependency ratio (above
      65 vs 15–64 years old) in China, from 1990–2018   134
5.3   Residential CO_2 emissions from electricity generation
      with projected urbanization rates (2008–2050)   135
5.4   Changes of average time spent by activities in China
      from 2018 to 2050 with projected urbanization rates,
      following the 2008 and 2018 time-use lifestyles   136
5.5   Change of annual residential CO_2 emissions from
      electricity consumption with projected urbanization
      rates between 2018 and 2050, following the 2008 and
      2018 time-use lifestyles   137

5.6   Population by age groups   138
5.7   Residential CO_2 emissions from electricity consump-
      tion with projected age profiles from 15 to 74 years
      old, following 2008 time-use lifestyle   138
5.8   Residential CO_2 emissions from electricity consump-
      tion with projected age profiles from 15 to 74 years
      old, following 2018 time-use lifestyle   139
5.9   Change of average time spent by activities in China
      from 2020 to 2050 with projected age profiles from age
      15 to 74 years old, following the 2008 and 2018 time-
      use lifestyles   140
5.10 Change of residential CO_2 emissions from electricity
      consumption with projected age profiles from age 15
      to 74 between 2020 and 2050, following the 2008 and
      2018 time-use lifestyles   140
5.11 Time use and CO_2 intensity effects on the differences of
      residential CO_2 emissions in 2008 and 2018 by activities   142
5.12 CO_2 intensity effects on the differences of residential
      CO_2 emissions from electricity consumption between
      2008 and 2018, by appliance operation mode   142
5.13 Time-use effects on the differences in residential CO_2
      emissions from electricity consumption between 2008
      and 2018, by appliance operation mode   143
5.14 Reductions of residential CO_2 emissions by appliance
      operation mode with one more hour more per day
      doing outdoor activities in 2008 and 2018   144
5.15 Share of residential CO_2 reduction by activity and
      appliance operation mode with an additional hour per
      day doing outdoor activities in 2008   145
5.16 Share of residential CO_2 reduction by activity and
      appliance operation mode with an additional hour per
      day doing outdoor activities in 2018   145
6.1 CO_2 emissions from the residential sector by fuel in 2008   149
6.2 CO_2 emissions from the residential sector by fuel in 2018   149

Tables

2.1   Demographic distribution of respondents sampled in
2008 and 2018 CTUS   34

2.2   Variables lists of Personal Information and Diary Episode   35

2.3   Activity categorization in this study and related
categories in 2008 and 2018 CTUS   36

3.1   Methods for estimating energy intensity of time use   71

3.2   Activity-appliance matching   73

3.3   List of variables in the 2012 Chinese Residential
Energy Consumption Survey   80

3.4   Population distribution by province in the 2012
Chinese Residential Energy Consumption Survey and
the 2012 annual national sample surveys of population   81

3.5   Profile of household characteristics in the 2012
Chinese Residential Energy Consumption Survey and
the 2012 annual national sample surveys of population   81

3.6   Appliance variables collected in the 2012 Chinese
Residential Energy Consumption Survey   98

Preface

Three decades have passed since the 1992 Earth Summit in Rio de Janeiro and the signature of the United Nations Convention on Climate Change (UNFCCC). The world certainly has gone a long way on the understanding of climate change and the determination to deal with it. The recent progress of the Paris Agreement has been witnessing a great majority of global greenhouse gases emissions under various forms of carbon neutrality commitments, or net zero emissions, especially in the two years preceding the 26th Conference of the Parties (COP26) of UNFCCC in October/November 2021.

A country or region's absolute carbon dioxide (CO_2) emissions can be decomposed into the product of two key factors, being GDP and carbon intensity. GDP indicates the size of the economy, and larger economies tend to emit more CO_2 to illustrate the *scale effect*. Carbon intensity measures CO_2 emissions per unit of GDP. GDP can be further broken down by sectors and different sectors have different carbon intensities. These absolute and intensity terms are also the two primary types that countries adopted for their individual CO_2 mitigation commitments, while the rapidly spreading carbon neutrality goals and their progress trajectories are mainly about absolute emissions.

For a country like China that witnessed its GDP being nearly 40 times larger in the past 40 years, *the scale effect* dominates the change of CO_2 emissions. It dwarfs the impacts of other significant changes, such as economic structure, energy efficiency and conservation, and energy transition. One of the authors (Xu) has been trying for long to seek an alternative perspective to look into the influential factors of CO_2 emissions without the scale effect and thus better distinguish other effects. Although GDP can grow larger and a person can become richer, the number of hours in a day can never be wound differently and thus no scale effect will be present.

Our quest of a more sustainable lifestyle is another lead of this study. In the running toward the Earth Summit, President George H. W. Bush of the United States once said famously: "The American way of life is not up for negotiations. Period." The world also clearly realizes that if the 1.4 billion residents in China had the "American way of life", the Earth would experience dangerous climate crises. The time-use and CO_2 intensity of various daily activities in 24 hours can quantitatively illustrate lifestyles to provide a perspective for understanding how sustainable or unsustainable they are and how to inch closer to sustainability.

Since the first author (Wong) was an undergraduate and then MPhil student, we have been collaborating to explore the linkage between time use and energy consumption as well as CO_2 emissions. This book updates our progress in this direction during the past half a dozen years and attempts to lay an initial steppingstone for this novel direction of research.

We are thankful to Professor Wei Chu of Renmin University of China for providing us with the microdata of the Chinese Residential Energy Consumption Survey and to the National Bureau of Statistics of China for the microdata of the Chinese Time-Use Survey. They form pivotal data foundations for this study.

We are also grateful for the support of our families, especially in the prolonged COVID-19 pandemic. Wong would like to express her gratitude to her family, Wai Sing Wong, Yuk Ying Lau, Pui Ki Wong, and Pak Tun Wong, for their unconditional support of her academic pursuits. Her thanks also go to her two adopted furry children, Tabasco and Soya, for keeping her company during those endless nights of writing.

Xu owes a big debt to his wife, Song Jing, a sociologist. Discussion with her was crucial to zoom into time use for achieving the above two purposes. Their two lovely children, Xu Anlan and Song Antao, have been growing rapidly over the course of writing this book. They are his beacon of light when the study runs into difficulty.

1 Introduction

1.1 Climate change and China's residential sector

Climate change is exerting far-reaching impacts around the world, and it should be the most expensive environmental crisis that has ever been encountered by humankind. Its key cause is the emissions of greenhouse gases, especially carbon dioxide (CO_2) from fossil fuel consumption. The Intergovernmental Panel on Climate Change (IPCC) has illustrated the urgency of reducing CO_2 emissions to zero as early as 2040 for controlling the global temperature increase below 1.5°C (IPCC, 2018, 2021). Climate change incurs huge economic and social damage, and its mitigation competes for financial resources away from other important issues.

China is a crucial stakeholder in climate change, currently being the largest CO_2-emitting country in the world. In the past three decades, China has experienced a 180-degree change of its climate change position. When the Kyoto Protocol was negotiated in 1997, China insisted upon the "common but differentiated responsibilities" that was written into the 1992 United Nations Framework Convention on Climate Change and refused to take on any legally binding goal. It emitted less CO_2 than the European Union and its per-capita emissions were not only just a fraction of developed economies but also much lower than the global average (Figures 1.1 and 1.2). In 2009 when China prepared itself for the incoming Copenhagen negotiation, the original position started to thaw, and the first CO_2 mitigation goal was announced to reduce CO_2 intensity (CO_2 emissions per unit of GDP) by 20–25% in 2020 from the 2005 level. At that moment, China's CO_2 emissions had already surpassed the United States to become the world largest (Figure 1.1). Even more importantly, its per-capita emissions were then higher than the global average (Figure 1.2). The Paris Agreement marked China's fundamental shift with a commitment

DOI: 10.4324/9780429291708-1

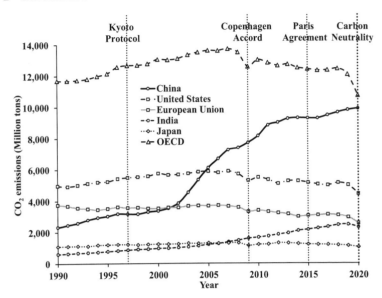

Figure 1.1 CO$_2$ emissions and key milestones.

(BP, 2021)

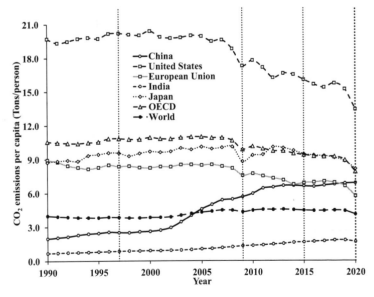

Figure 1.2 CO$_2$ emissions per capita.

(BP, 2021)

to reach peak emissions around 2030, while in 2020 this commitment was further strengthened with a carbon neutrality target for 2060. In 2020, China's CO_2 emissions were inching closer to the overall level from all OECD (Organization for Economic Co-operation and Development) countries, or the entire developed world with 1.3 billion people (Figure 1.1). An average Chinese then emitted more than an average European and was close to the OECD average, although still much lower than an average American (Figure 1.2).

China is the world's largest energy consumer. In 2020, it accounted for 26.1% of global primary energy consumption and a rare 2.1% growth when the world registered 4.5% reduction in the Covid-19 pandemic (BP, 2021). In conjunction with its economic development in recent decades, China's primary energy consumption has grown rapidly, from 603 million tons of coal equivalent (Mtce) in 1980 to 4875 Mtce in 2019 (Figure 1.3) (National Bureau of Statistics, 2016). At the same time, its energy mix has been gradually evolving with the increasing importance of primary electricity especially in the forms of renewables, from 8.4% in 2011 to 15.3% in 2019 (Figure 1.4). The most carbon-intensive fuel, coal, is still dominant in China, being 57.5% of

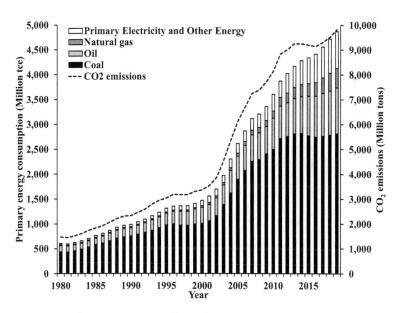

Figure 1.3 Primary energy consumption and CO_2 emissions in China (1980–2019).

(BP, 2020; National Bureau of Statistics, 2021)

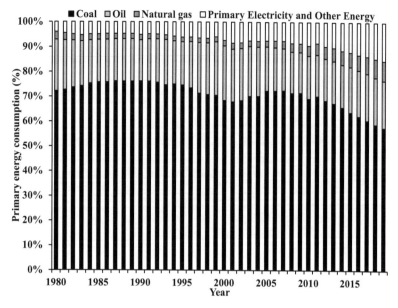

Figure 1.4 Fuel mix of China's primary energy consumption (1980–2019).
(National Bureau of Statistics, 2021)

the total in 2019, but its share has been dropping rapidly from 70.2% in 2011 (Figure 1.4). The overall consumption of coal has been stabilized in the recent decade, while China's economic growth still demands more energy consumption that is increasingly satisfied by non-coal, and especially non-fossil, fuels (Figure 1.3).

China is under high pressure to mitigate CO_2 emissions. In comparison with developed economies, a key feature of China is that its CO_2 emissions and energy consumption have not reached peaks. With the continuous CO_2 mitigation and spreading carbon neutrality commitments mostly for 2050, developed countries would witness the share of their annual CO_2 emissions decreasing steadily in the coming decade, while China's importance would keep rising even if the country can achieve the peak emission goal in 2030. From then, only three decades will be available to clean up CO_2 emissions to reach net zero in 2060.

As China rapidly has been industrialized, the secondary sector has continued dominating energy consumption with a share of 68.0% in 2019, while the primary and tertiary sectors accounted for 1.8% and

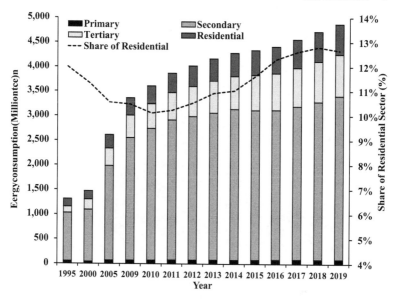

Figure 1.5 Energy consumption by sector.

(National Bureau of Statistics, 2021)

17.5%, respectively (Figure 1.5). The residential sector took a share of 12.7% in 2019, up from 10.1% in 2010 (Figure 1.5). It indicates that this sector alone now emits well over one billion tons of CO_2 to be ranked as the fifth largest emitter among countries after China itself, United States, India and Russia, and ahead of Japan.

Energy consumption in the residential sector has been continuously rising and electrified. In the past four decades since China's economic reform started, the residential energy consumption per person increased more than fourfold, while electricity consumption rose nearly seventy fold from merely 11 kWh in 1980 to 115 kWh in 2000 and 761 kWh in 2019 (Figures 1.6 and 1.7). Electricity was responsible for 64.3% of total residential energy consumption in 2019, up from just 4.2% in 1980 and 36.1% in 2000 (Figure 1.6). Fast electrification elevates the residential sector's importance in China's overall electricity consumption from 3.6% in 1980 to 10.8% in 2000 and then to 14.2% in 2019. Accordingly, China's residential electricity consumption results in about the same amount of CO_2 emissions as the whole of Germany. In addition, residential coal consumption per person was reduced by 60.2% from 1980 to 2019,

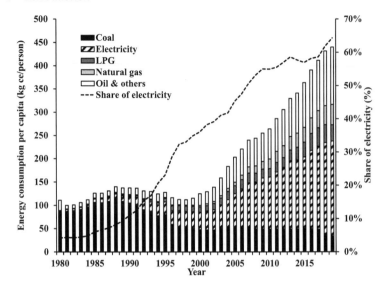

Figure 1.6 Residential energy consumption in China (1980–2019).

(National Bureau of Statistics, 2021)

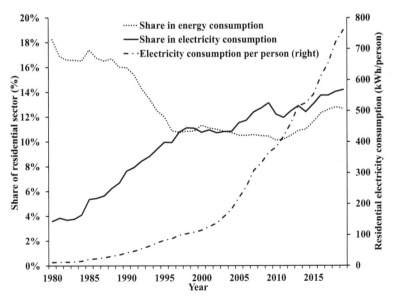

Figure 1.7 Residential electricity consumption and its shares in China (1980–2019).

(National Bureau of Statistics, 2021)

indicating that China's households are now consuming much cleaner fuels with much less concern about indoor air pollution. Studies have suggested that this evolution resulted from the interaction between urbanization, growth in income, improvement in appliance efficiency, and better insulation of residential buildings (Zhou et al., 2013).

1.2 Lifestyle and residential energy consumption

Lifestyles are closely related to energy consumption and CO_2 emissions (Wei, Liu, Fan, & Wu, 2007). How people conduct their daily life activities is correlated with the amount of energy needed and CO_2 emitted to provide the goods and services that they desire. Thus, since the 1970s, the term *lifestyle* has been widely employed in energy consumption studies and used to refer to the patterned variations in energy consumption and behavioral differences within a particular social group (Lutzenhiser, 1993).

1.2.1 Residential energy consumption

The analyses at household and individual levels adopted bottom-up approaches and addressed the issues of energy use from social and behavioral perspectives. These studies generally perceived energy consumption as the consequence of personal lifestyle and technology efficiency, while other factors like the stage of economic development and accessibility to electricity only indirectly affected energy use via its impacts on either individual lifestyle or energy efficiency (Sanquist, Orr, Shui, & Bittner, 2012; Wei et al., 2007). By quantifying lifestyle as consumption expenditure, several tools were developed to investigate impacts of consumption patterns on energy consumption.

Noting the limits of a conventional sector-based approach in linking energy consumption with actual individual lifestyle, Bin and Dowlatabadi (2005) proposed a paradigm that they called the *consumer lifestyle approach* (CLA) and utilized energy expenditure to explore the implications of individual lifestyles on energy consumption and related CO_2 emissions. Model results from their study indicated that consumer demand and related economic activities accounted for more than 80% of national energy consumption in the United States. The study also highlighted the importance of indirect energy consumption, showing that energy consumed for purposes such as food production, transport operations, and housing operation was twice as much as direct energy use for personal travel and housing. Following the approach of Bin and Dowlatabadi (2005), Wei et al. (2007) employed CLA for China to quantify the direct and indirect impacts of urban and rural residential lifestyles on energy consumption and associated CO_2 emissions from 1999 to 2002; and found that the residents' lifestyles related and economic activities accounted for 26% and 30% of annual national energy consumption and CO_2 emissions, respectively. In addition, a distinct difference was detected between urban and rural residents. For urban dwellers, the indirect effects were 2.44 times as high as the direct effects, while the ratio was only 1.86 times for rural residents. This variation was explained as a consequence of the lifestyle variation between urban and rural residents, particularly with regard to the fuel and devices used for cooking.

Studies have also been conducted with alternative approaches, such as the input-output approach and household survey, to understand the environmental impacts of household and individual lifestyles. Using the input-output approach, Ding, Cai, Wang, and Sanwal (2017) explored direct and indirect impacts of household lifestyles on energy consumption in China in 2012. They reported that 24.7% of national energy consumption could be attributed to consumers' activities, and the ratio of indirect effect to direct effect to be 1.35. In the use of household survey, Ouyang and Hokao (2009) explored the links between lifestyle and electricity consumption. They found that despite technological advancement, improved living standards and higher dependence on electric appliances would bring an on-going increase in residential energy consumption, and concluded that occupants' behavior at home would be the most crucial determinant for household energy consumption. A similar study has been conducted by Guerra Santin (2011), using household survey data to investigate the impacts of occupants' lifestyles and behavioral patterns on energy consumption for heating an urban household. It also yielded the similar result, stating that occupants' behavior, such as frequency of appliance use and practices to save energy, were pivotal in determining the amount of energy consumed for heating in the residential sector.

Other statistical methods like IPAT model, index decomposition analysis (IDA) and factor analysis were also employed in identifying non-behavioral determinants of household energy consumption and CO_2 emission (Feng, Hubacek, & Guan, 2009; Zha, Zhou, & Zhou, 2010). The STochastic Impacts by Regression on Population, Affluence and Technology (STIRPAT model), an upgraded version of IPAT equation, has been often employed in examining anthropo-genic sources of GHGs and their effects on the environment. It is a comprehensive approach, incorporating social, physical, and biological factors into consideration, as well as a strong tool for generating empirical evidences for policy making (Shahbaz, Loganathan, Muzaffar, Ahmed, & Ali Jabran 2016). In the recent decade, it has been also extended to examine the driving factors for energy consumption and related CO_2 emissions. In studies of China several scholars have used the STIRPAT model with urbanization--a board and rapid economic, social, and ecological transition--included as a drivers. Xu and Lin (2015) and Poumanyvong and Kaneko (2010) investigated the impacts of urbanization and industrialization on energy consumption and CO_2 emissions at the country level, while Ji and Chen (2017), Wang et al. (2017), and Wang, Wu, Zhu, and Wei (2013) have focused at the provincial level. These studies have collec-tively shown that urbanization in general, mainly represented by share of urban population, increased energy consumption and CO_2 emissions in China and in other regions.

Consumption-based studies , however, did not account two other important lifestyle factors: patterns of time and location of every-day activities. Schipper, Bartlett, Hawk, and Vine (1989) highlighted the importance of incorporating time in modeling residential energy demand, with three temporal aspects. First, the timing of everyday activities like the duration should be used as the ground to assess individual everyday lifestyles and assoicated energy consumption. Second, the time constraints imposed by social practices like formal working hours and opening hours of stores should be accounted to determine the kevek of synchronicity. Third, the energy rebound, loss in energy efficiency saving, from time saving activities needs to be considered for better estimations of residential energy consump-tion. Based on these factors, Schipper et al. (1989) concluded that "Models of future activity based on traditional economic analysis of expenditures, or estimation of energy demand as a function of prices and incomes alone, will miss this expanding range of what and how."

1.2.2 Urbanization and residential energy consumption

Individual lifestyle varies by demographic features such as gender and age, and by the external social environments to which people are exposed. Since industrialization and globalization, human landscapes have been unprecedentedly transformed by concurrent trends of modernization and urbanization. The typical lifestyles in today's world are sharply different from those a few decades ago, with more than half of the global population now residing in cities. In the coming decades, it is expected to have further urbanization with fundamental impacts on energy consumption. Deepening urbanization and overall population growth are projected to add 2.5 billion inhabitants to cities by 2050, with almost 90% in Asia and Africa, and the urbanization rate is expected to reach 66% by 2050 (United Nations, 2015). The more energy-intensive lifestyles of city dwellers could pose serious concerns about energy security and climate mitigation. With just half of the global population, cities will consume 67% of energy and emit 71% of CO_2 (International Energy Agency, 2008; United Nations, 2015). The rural-urban contrast in energy consumption varies among countries. In developing countries (with urbanization rate of 40% to 50%), per-capita residential energy use tends to be significantly higher in urban areas than rural areas, while there is not much difference in developed countries (International Energy Agency, 2008). Zheng et al. (2014) conducted a comprehensive survey at the household level in China and found that electricity, natural gas, and district heating were the three primary energy sources utilized in residential places, while the three main end-use activities were water heating, cooking, and space heating. In addition, a massive gap was revealed between energy use in urban centers verse rural regions. Space heating was mostly commercialized in urban areas, while the use of biomass was dominant in rural regions.

Even after three decades of rapid progress, China will continue to be critically important in further urbanization (United Nations, 2015). In 2019, 60.6% of Chinese citizens were urban, up from 19.4% in 1980 to 36.2% in 2000 (National Bureau of Statistics, 2021). China's CO_2 emissions have already been at the top of the world, while how it further urbanizes could have serious implications for global climate mitigation efforts. The causal relationship between urbanization and energy use has been extensively investigated in recent decades using various types of data and models at national and city levels. Most of the empirical findings revealed a positive link between urbanization and energy use (Alam, Fatima, & Butt, 2007; Jones, 1991); however, it was not universally applicable to all regions and sectors (e.g., Liddle, 2004; Mishra, Smyth, & Sharma, 2009; Newman & Kenworthy, 1996). Some suggested that these conflicting results were due to the heterogeneity across regions. At the national level, Poumanyvong and Kaneko (2010) found that the impacts of urbanization on energy consumption varied across the stages of development, with level of urbanization was positively correlated to energy use in the middle- and high-income countries, but negatively associated in low-income countries. UNFPA (2016) also argued that in developing country can help enhancing environmental sustainability by promoting better utilization of resources and boosting the development of a green economy. Even within the same countries, Zhang and Lin (2012) and Wang, Wu, Zeng, and Wu (2016) have respectively identified significant differences in the extent to which urbanization affects energy use between eastern, central and western China and among provinces. They argued that China has undergone a negative and non-linear relationship between urbanization, energy consumption, and CO_2 emissions as stated in the "urban environment transition theory." The increase in the urbanization rate in major cities like Shanghai and Beijing has led to an increase in energy consumption due to the growth in demand for energy services in public and private residential sectors, while in western and central China, a positive association between urbanization and energy consumption was caused by its development of industries with low energy efficiency. In eastern China, urbanization and energy consumption were, however, decoupled owning to the dominant development of energy-efficient light industries (Wang et al., 2016).

Similar variations in the causal relationship between urbanization and energy consumption were also observed in comparative study of 99 countries with different level of urbanization conducted by Poumanyvong and Kaneko (2010), Despite the general positive relationship between urbanization and CO2 emission, they found that the direction of the effect varied across different income groups. In high- and middle-income countries, urbanization was associated with increased energy consumption, while in low-income countries, it led to a decrease in energy consumption.

Apart from studies investigating the direction and strength of the causal relationship between urbanization and energy consumption, scholars have also sought to explain the relationship. In China, to respond to the announcement of the ambitious New-Type Urbanization Plan, Elliott, Sun, and Zhu (2017) explored the direct and indirect effects of urbanization on energy consumption in construction, industrial upgrading, changing lifestyles, and transportation , and correlated them with residents' behaviors between 1995 and 2012 across 33 provinces in China. The direct effects were found to be positive; however, indirect effects were found to be negative in all four end-uses. Combining both direct and indirect effects, a percentage increase in the floating urban population would lead to an increase of 0.753% to 1.473% in coal and electricity consumption, respectively (Elliott et al., 2017). Ding and Li (2017) also investigated the positive impact of urbanization on CO_2 emissions through analysing changes in economic structures and income across provinces in China from 2000 to 2013. Using logarithmic mean Divisia index approach, they concluded that along with urbanization, economic factors -- GDP and household income -- were the more dominant contributors than other factors like social transitions, energy intensity, and structural changes.

Studies have also explored the relationship between urbanization and energy consumption in residential sector. Donglan, Dequn, and Peng (2010) estimated and compared the levels of emissions related to energy use within rural and urban residential sectors from 1991 to 2004, and found that population growth was the major contributor to the increase in residential energy use and CO_2 emissions in urban China, while decrease in population and insignificant economic development have consistently reduced residential CO_2 emissions in rural areas Zhao, Li, and Ma (2012) , while, focused on household level and concluded that shape changes in urban residential energy consumption were associated with the increasing use of energy-intensive appliances and equipment. some contrastive changes were also observed. A gradual transition towards less CO_2 intensive energy, such as natural gas, oil and electricity was observed in urban Chinese, reflecting an increasing awareness to environmental protection, comfort, and convenience. The increase in energy price was also found to significant contribute to the reduction in residential energy consumption. These studies have provide extensive observations and detailed explanations to the causal relationship between urbanization and energy consumption. However, most of these studies were limited to aggregate levels, and the contribution of everyday lifestyle, as highlighted by Schipper et al. (1989), was often overlooked.

1.2.3 Demographic change and residential energy consumption

The global backdrop of population growth and demographic composition are directly related to residential energy consumption. The world has been undergoing dramatic demographic transition since the nineteenth century. The first demographic transition brought down the mortality rate, and later the second demographic transition many countries have been experiencing is characterized by the sub-replacement fertility rate (Van de Kaa, 1987). One of the most influential consequences was that many countries have been facing an increasingly older population profile and an increasing spatial mobility of individuals. The urbanizing world is also aging rapidly to expect 2.1 billion people at the age 60 or above (21.3% in total population) in 2050, while nearly four fifths will be living in developing countries with China accounting for 479 million (United Nations, 2017a). As people age on a large scale, their lifestyles change accordingly. Consequently, an aging population is relevant to energy consumption in multiple ways. Older populations are associated with smaller household size (Liu, Daily, Ehrlich, & Luck, 2003), which is an important predictor of residential energy use. Also, in comparison to the working-age population, old people tend to consume more energy at home but less energy for transportation (Liddle, 2014; O'Neill & Chen, 2002) and especially driving cars (York, 2003). Older people can consume more energy for various reasons. Older people do not possess sufficient knowledge of energy problems and solutions, are less inclined to use environmental-friendly measures, demand more comfortable heating and cooling conditions that consume more energy, and live in older dwellings (Abrahamse & Steg, 2011; Nair, Gustavsson, & Mahapatra, 2010; Poortinga, Steg, Vlek, & Wiersma, 2003; Stern, 2000). Nevertheless, the empirical inquiry of whether aging increases or decreases energy consumption is far less conclusive (Frederiks, Stenner, & Hobman, 2015) and requires more evidence in the concrete cultural context. Another aspect of this inquiry is whether the association between age and energy consumption is linear or curvilinear. The consumption of energy can reach the peak in mid-life, then decline later because the mid-life is often associated with large household size (Fritzsche, 1981); or conversely, it is the younger and older household that are the most demanding of energy as the middle-aged individuals are more likely to be energy-savers (Stern, 2000). Regardless of the lack of conclusive evidence, aging societies pose challenges for governments, policy makers, and other relevant stakeholders.

Gender is another critical demographic factor to affect residential energy consumption (Permana, Abd Aziz, & Siong, 2015; Raty & Carlsson-Kanyama, 2010). From a theoretical perspective, the socialization of gender roles is influential in shaping individuals' attitudes towards environmental issues. Previous studies consistently indicated that women held more pro-environmental attitudes and values than men (Dietz, Kalof, & Stern, 2002; Hunter, Hatch, & Johnson, 2004) because cultural norms of acceptable social roles differ by gender; women are socialized to be caring, nursing, and altruistic, and they extend the protective values to environments (Blocker & Eckberg, 1997; Stern, Dietz, & Kalof, 1993). The environmentally friendly values held by women will render them pro-environment energy users. In accordance with differentiated values, there is a gendered pattern of energy consumption. Women tend to save energy in everyday life. Family studies literature has long suggested that the division of labor in the nuclear family is gendered across cultures (Altintas & Sullivan, 2016; Craig & Mullan, 2010). In general, men spend more time in the labor market and women spend more time in the private sphere. Women spend less time on commuting between home and workplace (Crane, 2007) and consequently, they are less frequent users of driving. The different patterns of time use are also associated with how individuals consume energy; women are mainly responsible for the use of home appliances and managing electricity consumption at home (Tjørring, Jensen, Hansen, & Andersen, 2018). Additionally, considering the important roles of fertility behaviors (Pollmann-Schult, 2017), and employment (Chen, 2005) in the gendered division of labor in the household, these life course events and beyond all add to the complexity of the effect of gender on energy consumption insides the household. Moreover, even within the single household, men tend to incur more energy consumption for transportation (Raty & Carlsson-Kanyama, 2010) and women often make better energy decisions in the residential sector (Permana et al., 2015). The evolving gender imbalance and improving gender equality could yield profound impacts on energy consumption across countries (United Nations, 2017b).

1.3 Time use as a residential lifestyle indicator

1.3.1 Time-use survey and applications

Time-use survey is an important indicator of lifestyle other than consumption expenditure, as stated by United Nations Department of Economic and Social Affairs (2005)—"a common source using a common unit of measure for fundamental descriptive data not otherwise obtainable on human activities in various fields of social, demographic and related economic statistics". It provides quantitative measures of how individuals allocate the hours in the days to activities and is an important tool for dealing with a wide range of policy issues, such as leisure, healthcare, and transportation. It has also been used in academia to explore topics like social changes, household obligations, and division of labor, as well as quantification of the value of housework.

Time-use survey has a long history of development. It was first designed and used by Bevans in 1913 to collect data on workingmen's welfare (Szalai, 1974). Later, its field of application was expanded; small-scale surveys were conducted by scholars to investigate topics like women's activities in rural areas and the impacts of technological advances on the activity patterns of housewives. The first large-scale time-use survey was conducted in the 1920s by Russian economists with the financial support of the government to uncover the impacts of the cultural revolution on the lives of industrial workers in Moscow (Szalai, 1974). Since then, more countries, including the United States, the former Soviet Union, and the United Kingdom, have conducted time-use surveys to assess people's livelihoods. In the latest decades, with the development of computers, it has even been included as regular national statistics in countries like the United States for gathering data to formulate social policies. Apart from the effort in government statistical offices, another crucial driver for the development of time-use survey has been the establishment of the Multinational Time-Use Study. It unified the otherwise disparate time-use surveys to create a unified diary layout and an information-gathering procedure. This has then attracted a group of scholars to conduct follow-up studies (Michelson, 2015). One of them was Philip Stone at the Murray Centre at Radcliffe College, who later founded the Working Group on Time Budgets and Social Activities in 1970. This group has later become the largest time use-related association: the International Association for Time-Use Research (IATUR, 2018).

Currently, time-use surveys have been conducted in over 85 countries worldwide (United Nations, 2016). They were in the range of medium- to large-scale with sample sizes of 3,000 to 25,000, and were either as a stand-alone survey or a module in a household survey (Charmes, 2017). They were generally collected through household interviews and/or computer-assisted telephone interviews. As for the survey instruments and activity classification methods, they were mostly consistent with, or similar to, the international classification schemes like the Harmonised Activity Classification for Time-Use Surveys in Europe by Eurostat and International Classification of Activities for Time-Use Statistics by the United Nations. However, the American Time-Use Survey has its own classification scheme.

In academia, time-use survey data have been primarily employed by sociologists to assess social well-being (Michelson, 2015). Most of the studies were conducted in Western countries and analyzed the American Time-Use Survey or Harmonized European Time-Use Survey. The most studied topic was the value of unpaid housework, as its importance was emphasized earlier by the United Nations (1996) that "developing methods quantifying the value of unremunerated work that is outside national accounts, such as caring for dependents and preparing food, for possible reflection in satellite accounts" (p. 87). One of the most cited studies was Landefeld and McCulla (2000)'s valuation method, which estimated the value of unpaid work based on time-series population data by gender and participation rate in economic activity, compensation of employees, and American time-use survey data. They concluded that if the unpaid housework was included in the calculation, the GDP in the United States would be 43% and 24% higher in 1946 and 1997 than the results obtained with the conventional method. Using the same approach, Michelson (2015) further extended to quantify the value of the work of consumer services professionals, managers and scientists, services workers, and manual workers; and found that these additional items could collectively add 39% additional GDP. Therefore, the time-use scholars argued that the conventional economic indicators have greatly underestimated the value of the output value of unpaid housework and service sector.

Time-use surveys were also often used to explore the public health topics, such as the involvement in sleeping and physical activity, and to identify their demographic determinants. By analyzing the 2003–2005 ATUS, Basner et al. (2007) revealed a causal relationship between the amount of sleep and individuals' other daily activities in the United States. They reported negative correlations of sleep with work time, commute time, and leisure time, with an additional hour of sleep over the average of 7.5 hours/day was associated with 37.1 minutes less on working, 7 minutes less on commuting, or 5 minutes less on leisure activities. Also, by analyzing the same set of time-use data Catrine, Washington, Ainsworth, and Troiano (2009) revealed that Americans who spent about 11 hours/day on occupational and non occupational sedentary tasks tended to engage in far less than the recommended level of physical activity.

The third sociological topic discussed in the use of time-use survey data was quality of life. However, in order to analyze this topic, a special type of time-use survey with an additional column in the time-use diary is needed to record respondents' feelings (e.g., positive, negative, and tired), namely the day reconstruction method. It was first introduced by Kahneman, Krueger, Schkade, Schwarz, and Stone (2004) to assess individual well-being . It examines how people spend their time and what their experiences are during various activities in different settings of their daily lives. Kahneman et. al (2004) carried out a small-scale survey of 909 respondents in the United States and found that life satisfaction was related to the daily net effect between positive and negative episodes during a day, as well as to demographic factors like marital status and personal characteristics such as personality and temperament. In a follow-up study, they shifted the focus to the relationship between income and subjective happiness, and surprisingly, found that the common perception that wealth leads to greater happiness may not be correct. People with an above-average income may be relatively more satisfied with their lives, but are not happier than the lower-income groups because they fail to spend time on enjoyable activities due to heavier institutional activity constraints (Kahneman, Krueger, Schkade, Schwarz, & Stone, 2006)

In China, only a few empirical studies have analyzed time-use survey data for the above topics. Based on the first Chinese time-use survey in 2008, Zhou, Li, Xue, and Lei (2010) revealed that the amount of time spent on subsistence activities was positively correlated to leisure activities, but negatively correlated to maintenance activities. The ratio of these three groups of activities was reported to be 60:24:16, which was notably distinct from that of other countries. Another empirical example was Schwanen and Wang (2014). They used their own time-use diary collected in Hong Kong to analyze the relationship of well-being with geographical context, social contacts, and life circumstances, and concluded that the geographic context, the activity location, was crucial for overall daily well-being and moment-to-moment experiences.

1.3.2 *Time use and energy consumption*

"The ways in which people view and use time have very real material consequences that both shape and reflect the relationship between human society and the physical environment" (Rau, 2015, p. 373). This statement brings out the importance of including time-use patterns when studying the environmental impacts of human society. In fact, after Schipper et al. (1989) first emphasized the importance of time-use patterns in studying energy consumption, more attentions were drawn to conduct energy studies from time-use perspective. These studies could be generally divided into two groups: (i) developing bottom-up residential electricity demand models; and (ii) investigating how energy consumption is embedded directly and indirectly in individual lifestyles.

Time-use data are considered as indicators of occupants' behaviors in the context of developing bottom-up residential electricity demand models in the first group of studies. Capsso, Grattieri, Lamedica, and Prudenzi (1994) pioneered the construction of a bottom-up model employing time-use data. In their model, residential electricity loads were simulated on an hourly interval based on time-use data (indicators of occupants' behaviors) and installed appliances characteristics (indicators of technical dimension of occupants' energy-consuming behaviors). Thereafter, coupled with the increasing awareness of demand-side management and more publications of time-use surveys, numerous empirical studies have been conducted to improve the accuracy and precision of these bottom-up modeling approaches. Of these studies, two have been the most influential. The first was by Richardson, Thomson, Infield, and Clifford (2010), who proposed a high-resolution model of residential electricity consumption based on the active occupancy patterns and the daily activity patterns derived from time-use data. Based on the 2000 UK time-use data, the model simulated a residential electricity profile with a resolution of one-minute , with results well validated against the actual annual average electricity load measured in a small sample of 22 dwellings in a community in the East Midlands. Using a similar approach, Torriti (2012), Marszal-Pomianowska, Heiselberg, and Kalyanova Larsen (2016), Fischer, Härtl, and Wille-Haussmann (2015) also succeeded in stimulated near-reality high-resolution household electricity profiles in Demark and Germany using time-use data from their respective countries. Another important study in bottom-up residential electricity demand modeling was Widén and Wäckelgård (2010). They placed additional emphasis on the technical dimensions of occupants' energy-consuming behaviors and incorporated the time-of-use characteristics of appliances into their model, namely consuming energy only during an activity, constantly throughout the day, or after the activity. This makes the simulation results further closer to reality. However, since this model has high requirements for data input, to our knowledge, no follow-up studies have been conducted. However, scholars such as Ramírez-Mendiola, Grünewald, and Eyre (2018) have questioned the accuracy of these bottom-up modeling results, arguing that the types of electric appliance used in the same activity can vary significantly throughout the day in the real world. Taking food preparation as an example, the energy intensity of the activity may vary considerably between meals, depending on the cooking appliances used. Breakfast tended to use less energy, as there were usually only short time uses of small kitchen appliances like kettles and toasters, while preparation of dinners often use energy-intensive appliances like ovens for longer periods of time. In addition to the bottom-up residential electricity demand modeling, other scholars have extended the application of these bottom-up models to assess the time-of-use dependence of electricity by end-use activity. Torriti (2017) revealed that the higher the time dependence of end-use activities, the greater its impacts on the peak electricity load. That, bathing/showering, which was found to have the highest dependence on time-of-use (mostly performed between 06:30 and 07:30 am), was the main cause of the sharp morning peak consumption in United Kingdom.

In the second group of time-use perspective energy studies, scholar have integrated time-use and consumption expenditure data to characterize the relationship between individual everyday lifestyle and material consumption (Heinonen, Jalas, Juntunen, Ala-Mantila, & Junnila, 2013b; Jalas, 2002, 2009, 2012; Jalas & Juntunen, 2015; Wiedenhofer, Smetschka, Akenji, Jalas, & Haberl, 2018). Jalas (2002) first introduced a time-use perspective to uncover the direct and indirect energy consumption embedded in individual daily lifestyles, based on the assumption that all material consumption is to fulfill the needs of individuals' everyday behaviors. Based on the data from the national time-use survey, household expenditure survey, and input-output table of Finland, they estimated the direct and indirect energy intensity of activity in Finnish two-person households and identified potential time-use rebound effects, which time and energy savings from eco-efficient goods and services were offset by shifts of saved time to other energy-intensive activities. As an extension of previous work, Jalas (2005) applied decomposition analysis to investigate the contributions of population growth, household types, time-use activities, energy intensities of activities, and household infrastructure on the changes in Finnish residential energy consumption from 1987–1990 to 1998–2000. The first two empirical studies led to a gradual consolidation of the approach, and in his third study, Jalas (2009) presented a revised design of "time use perspective on consumption" (p. 168), solidifying his view of residential energy consumption as the sum of product of amount of time spent on activities and energy intensities of activities.

Jalas and Juntunen (2015) repeated their studies on 2005 and decomposed the changes in direct and indirect energy consumption of Finnish households from 1987 to 2009 to examine the impacts of population growth, household types, time-use activities, energy intensities of activities, and non-allocated energy use. They found that the main reasons for the rise in energy consumption within the timeframe were the increase in infrastructure energy use and the rise in energy intensity of activities. The results also raised a concern that shifts in household type towards elderly couples and households without children may lead to a further increase in energy consumption, given that the average energy intensity of activities of these two household types was much higher than the others. The same approach was adopted by Druckman, Buck, Hayward, and Jackson (2012) for study the United Kingdom, and found that household everyday lives have directly and indirectly accounted for 75% of the UK carbon emissions.

Time-use perspective energy consumption studies have also been carried out to reveal the energy implications of the time-use patterns for residential electricity consumption in the context of social changes. Also for Finland, Heinonen, Jalas, Juntunen, Ala-Mantila, and Junnila (2013a) and Heinonen et al. (2013b) found that citizens living in different urban forms tended to have different time-use and energy consumption. An urban form could influence individual lifestyles in a variety of social aspects, such as commuting, social emulation and contacts, availability of goods and services, housing types, and pastime options. Consequently, these differences in lifestyles of individuals residing in different urban forms would be transformed into their differences in energy consumption and CO_2 emissions. Wiedenhofer et al. (2018) took the same view that household demographics and urban setting, through their impacts on time-use patterns, contributed to different emission types and intensities. They pointed out that since most of the emissions were directly or indirectly caused by individuals' everyday life, changing time-use lifestyles of individuals would be one of the most effective strategies to mitigate CO_2 emission.

Similiar studies have also been conducted in China, despite of the constraints of limited time-use data. Xu, Song, and Zhang (2014) estimated the energy consumption by activity for the United States and China based on their time-use, energy consumption, and population data, and decomposed the differences between the two countries into time-use and energy intensity effects. Their result was consistent with Jalas and Juntunen (2015) in Finland, having energy intensity effect as the main contributor to the d Yu, Wei, Kei, and Matsuoka (2018) narrowed its focus to residential sector in China and applied time-use data to its energy consumption and CO_2 emissions. They argued that although demographic transitions and population dynamics were widely accepted as the major causes for the increasing energy consumption and CO_2 emissions in China, their the underlying mechanism has not been clearly explained. In a case study in Sichuan, they suggested that with the inclusion of the potential associated changes in time-use pattern, the aging population and the reduction in household size would led to an enormous increase in energy consumption and CO_2 emission.

Different demographic transitions are currently occurring in both developing and developed countries worldwide. The transitions are characterized by changes in migration patterns, regional distribution, age structure, and the population size. To explore the connection between CO_2 emissions and individuals' everyday life is therefore an essential task to establish a ground for CO_2 mitigation. In China, although some studies attempted to utilize time-use data in the context of environmental issues, the attention placed was still limited.

1.4 Objectives and outline

This book aims to build a bridge between residential electricity consumption and its associated CO_2 emissions, on the one hand, and time-use patterns as lifestyles, on the other. The two academic research topics in energy studies and sociology have been only occasionally linked together. One key difficulty is that they have different statistical categories and thus datasets are often not matched. This book lays out the methodological foundation for this interdisciplinary research topic. The time-use survey data with daily activity and demographic details will be employed to reconstruct residential CO_2 emissions from electricity consumption with the same details. The new dataset could be analyzed for a much deeper understanding of how lifestyles and demographic characteristics influence residential CO_2 emissions through time use. China is taken as a case study to apply the methodology and empirically explore the research topic. China's households are contributing a significant and growing share of global CO_2 emissions. We will analyze their residential CO_2 intensities and emissions that arise from electricity consumption for various daily activities. Any reallocation of time from a more CO_2-intensive activity to a lower one will essentially reduce overall CO_2 emissions. In addition, we will discuss how to shape and revise people's voluntary time-use patterns for CO_2 mitigation.

We suggest a strategy for achieving more climate-friendly living. Individuals could be guided to voluntarily revise their time-use patterns. When a person spends more time in less-energy-intensive activity, his/her time budget for other activities, especially more-energy-intensive ones, will automatically be squeezed because the overall time budget is 24 hours, equal for everyone.

The following chapters are organized as follows. Chapter 2 examines how Chinese citizens spend a typical day on a variety of daily activities. Our data analysis will explore time-use patterns against various indicators, including urban/rural, age, gender, income, education level, economic status (retired, working, studying, etc.), household size, as well as weekdays/weekends. For example, rural Chinese on average work significant longer than urban Chinese. Women tend to shoulder more housework and thus spend more time at home than men. Old people stay home longer and use less time on transport. The two years of time-use survey data will also be utilized to understand how Chinese lifestyles changed. From 2008 to 2018, China had become more urbanized and wealthier. These demographic trends are expected to affect the time-use patterns of individuals and the whole society.

Corresponding to the daily activities that are discussed in the previous chapter, Chapter 3 is devoted to understanding residential electricity/CO_2 intensities (Watt/person or grams CO_2/hour/person). In performing a daily activity, certain electric appliances are utilized to consume electricity. However, no data are readily available on residential electricity intensities by daily activity. We will do the estimation with residential survey data and other statistics on the ownership of electric appliances and residents' behaviors. One person's daily residential electricity consumption (kWh/person/day, available in energy statistics) is understood as being incurred through conducting daily time-using activities (kWh/person/day for each activity, calculated through multiplying residential electricity intensity and time use). Because the latter bottom-up data and the former energy statistics data are independent from each other, the equation will be used to validate the estimation of residential electricity intensities for making adjustment and revision when necessary. With data on China's CO_2 emission factor of electricity, we will extend the research in understanding the CO_2 intensities of daily time-using activities. We will then analyze the residential CO_2 intensities and especially compare them across different daily activities. The quantitative assessment will rank daily activities and put them into high, medium, and low CO_2-intensive categories.

Different daily activities have different time-use and residential CO_2 intensities to result in different residential CO_2 emissions. Chapter 4 will examine and rank these activities in terms of their residential CO_2 emissions. The two years of time-use survey data allow longitudinal comparison. The daily residential CO_2 emissions will be further analysed corresponding to the demographic indicators. How time-use patterns shape the differences in residential CO_2 emissions will also be quantitatively studied. People with certain demographic indicators could use more time in activities with higher residential CO_2 intensities.

China's demographic changes will be first sketched in Chapter 5. The climate impacts of various demographic changes will be quantitatively studied. Because individuals differ from each other in residential CO_2 emissions as examined in Chapter 4, the overall or average residential CO_2 emissions will shift when the demographic profiles evolve. The Chinese society has been aging rapidly while old people tend to consume more residential electricity and emit more associated CO_2. The result is that the aging population profile leads to more residential CO_2 emissions for an average Chinese citizen. Rapid urbanization also exerts impacts on residential CO_2 emissions due to the differences in time-use patterns and residential CO_2 intensities of urban and rural residents. Scenarios of future demographic changes will be adopted from several key sources, including the Chinese government and the United Nations. Their impacts on residential CO_2 emissions will be projected. Furthermore, the potential climate impacts of time-use measures like encouraging participation in low carbon-intensive outdoor activities will also be discussed.

Chapter 6 concludes the entire book and explores how time use could be managed for helping control China's overall residential CO_2 emissions. Demographic profiles are hardly a deliberate policy target for the mitigation of greenhouse gases. If individuals could be attracted to voluntarily reduce time use for more CO_2 intensive activities, the saved time might be reallocated to other activities with lower CO_2 intensities and thus the overall CO_2 emissions of individuals would decrease. Urban planning for time management then will play a role in achieving more climate-friendly living, especially catering to the changing demographic profiles.

References

Abrahamse, W., & Steg, L. (2011). Factors related to household energy use and intention to reduce it: The role of psychological and socio-demographic variables. *Human Ecology Review*, *18*, 30–40.

Alam, S., Fatima, A., & Butt, M. S. (2007). Sustainable development in Pakistan in the context of energy consumption demand and environmental degradation. *Journal of Asian Economics, 18*(5), 825–837. doi: 10.1016/j.asieco.2007.07.005

Altintas, E., & Sullivan, O. (2016). Fifty years of change updated: Cross-national gender convergence in housework. *Demographic Research, 35*, 455–470.

Basner, M., Fomberstein, K. M., Razavi, F. M., Banks, S., William, J. H., Rosa, R. R., & Dinges, D. F. (2007). American time use survey: Sleep time and its relationship to waking activities. *Sleep, 30*(9), 1085–1095. doi: 10.1093/sleep/30.9.1085

Bin, S., & Dowlatabadi, H. (2005). Consumer lifestyle approach to US energy use and the related CO_2 emissions. *Energy Policy, 33*(2), 197–208. doi: 10.1016/S0301-4215(03)00210-6

Blocker, T. J., & Eckberg, D. L. (1997). Gender and environmentalism: Results from the 1993 general social survey. *Social Science Quarterly, 78*, 841–858.

BP. (2020). *Statistical Review of World Energy.* Retrieved from: https://www.bp.com/en/global/corporate/energy-economics/statistical-review-of-world-energy.html

BP. (2021). *Statistical Review of World Energy.* Retrieved from: https://www.bp.com/en/global/corporate/energy-economics/statistical-review-of-world-energy.html

Capsso, A., Grattieri, W., Lamedica, R., & Prudenzi, A. (1994). A bottom-up approach to residential load modeling. *IEEE Transactions on Power Systems, 9*(2). doi: 10.1109/59.317650

Catrine, T. L., Washington, T. L., Ainsworth, B. E., & Troiano, R. P. (2009). Linking the American time use survey (ATUS) and the compendium of physical activities: Methods and rationale. *Journal of Physical Activity and Health, 6*(3), 347–353.

Charmes, J. (2017). Time-use surveys in Africa: Problems and prospects. In Indira Hirway (Ed), *Mainstreaming unpaid work* (pp. 141–169). Oxford University Press.

Chen, F. A. (2005). Employment transitions and the household division of labor in China. *Social Forces, 84*(2), 831–851. doi: 10.1353/sof.2006.0010

Craig, L., & Mullan, K. (2010). Parenthood, gender and work-family time in the United States, Australia, Italy, France, and Denmark. *Journal of Marriage and Family, 72*, 1344–1361.

Crane, R. (2007). Is there a quiet revolution in women's travel? Revisiting the gender gap in commuting. *Journal of the American Planning Association, 73*, 298–316.

Dietz, T., Kalof, L., & Stern, P. C. (2002). Gender, values, and environmentalism. *Social Science Quarterly, 83*, 353–364.

Ding, Y., & Li, F. (2017). Examining the effects of urbanization and industrialization on carbon dioxide emission: Evidence from China's provincial regions. *Energy, 125*, 533–542. doi: 10.1016/j.energy.2017.02.156

Ding, Q., Cai, W., Wang, C., & Sanwal, M. (2017). The relationships between household consumption activities and energy consumption in china—An input-output analysis from the lifestyle perspective. *Applied Energy, 207,* 520–532. doi: 10.1016/j.apenergy.2017.06.003

Donglan, Z., Dequn, Z., & Peng, Z. (2010). Driving forces of residential CO_2 emissions in urban and rural China: An index decomposition analysis. *Energy Policy, 38*(7), 3377–3383. doi: 10.1016/j.enpol.2010.02.011

Druckman, A., Buck, I., Hayward, B., & Jackson, T. (2012). Time, gender and carbon: A study of the carbon implications of British adults' use of time. *Ecological Economics, 84,* 153–163. doi: 10.1016/j.ecolecon.2012.09.008

Elliott, R. J. R., Sun, P., & Zhu, T. (2017). The direct and indirect effect of urbanization on energy intensity: A province-level study for China. *Energy, 123,* 677–692. doi: 10.1016/j.energy.2017.01.143

Feng, K. S., Hubacek, K., & Guan, D. B. (2009). Lifestyles, technology and CO_2 emissions in China: A regional comparative analysis. *Ecological Economics, 69*(1), 145–154. Retrieved from <Go to ISI>://WOS:000271359400016 http://www.sciencedirect.com/science/article/pii/S0921800909003164

Fischer, D., Härtl, A., & Wille-Haussmann, B. (2015). Model for electric load profiles with high time resolution for German households. *Energy and Buildings, 92,* 170–179. doi: 10.1016/j.enbuild.2015.01.058

Frederiks, E. R., Stenner, K., & Hobman, E. V. (2015). The socio-demographic and psychological predictors of residential energy consumption: A comprehensive review. *Energies, 8,* 573–609.

Fritzsche, D. J. (1981). An analysis of energy consumption patterns by stage of family life cycle. *Journal of Marketing Research, 18,* 227–232.

Guerra Santin, O. (2011). Behavioural patterns and user profiles related to energy consumption for heating. *Energy and Buildings, 43*(10), 2662–2672. doi: 10.1016/j.enbuild.2011.06.024

Heinonen, J., Jalas, M., Juntunen, J. K., Ala-Mantila, S., & Junnila, S. (2013a). Situated lifestyles: I. How lifestyles change along with the level of urbanization and what the greenhouse gas implications are—A study of Finland. *Environmental Research Letters, 8*(2), 025003. doi: 10.1088/1748-9326/8/2/025003

Heinonen, J., Jalas, M., Juntunen, J. K., Ala-Mantila, S., & Junnila, S. (2013b). Situated lifestyles: II. The impacts of urban density, housing type and motorization on the greenhouse gas emissions of the middle-income consumers in Finland. *Environmental Research Letters, 8*(3), 035050. doi: 10.1088/1748-9326/8/3/035050

Hunter, L. M., Hatch, A., & Johnson, A. (2004). Cross-national gender variation in environmental behaviors. *Social Science Quarterly, 85*(3), 677–694. doi: 10.1111/j.0038-4941.2004.00239.x

IATUR. (2018). *About IATUR vzw.* Retrieved from https://www.iatur.org

International Energy Agency. (2008). *World Energy Outlook 2008.* Paris: http://www.worldenergyoutlook.org/media/weowebsite/2008-1994/weo2008.pdf

IPCC. (2018). *Global Warming of 1.5°C.* Retrieved from

IPCC. (2021). *Climate Change 2021: The Physical Science Basis*. Retrieved from

Jalas, M. (2002). A time use perspective on the materials intensity of consumption. *Ecological Economics, 41*(1), 109–123. doi: 10.1016/S0921-8009(02)00018-6

Jalas, M. (2005). The everyday life context of increasing energy demands: Time use survey data in a decomposition analysis. *Journal of Industrial Ecology, 9*(1–2), 129–145.

Jalas, M. (2009). Time-use rebound effects: An activity-based view of consumption. In H. Herring & S. Sorrell (Eds), *Energy efficiency and sustainable consumption*. London: Palgrave Macmillan.

Jalas, M. (2012). Debating the proper pace of life: Sustainable consumption policy processes at national and municipal levels. *Environmental Politics, 21*(3), 369–386. doi: 10.1080/09644016.2012.671570

Jalas, M., & Juntunen, J. K. (2015). Energy intensive lifestyles: Time use, the activity patterns of consumers, and related energy demands in Finland. *Ecological Economics, 113*, 51–59. doi: 10.1016/j.ecolecon.2015.02.016

Ji, X., & Chen, B. (2017). Assessing the energy-saving effect of urbanization in China based on stochastic impacts by regression on population, affluence and technology (STIRPAT) model. *Journal of Cleaner Production, 163*, S306–S314. doi: 10.1016/j.jclepro.2015.12.002

Jones, D. W. (1991). How urbanization affects energy-use in developing countries. *Energy Policy, 19*(7), 621–630.

Kahneman, D., Krueger, A. B., Schkade, D. A., Schwarz, N., & Stone, A. A. (2004). A survey method for characterizing daily life experience: The day reconstruction method. *Science, 306*(5702), 1776–1780. doi: 10.1126/science.1103572

Kahneman, D., Krueger, A. B., Schkade, D., Schwarz, N., & Stone, A. A. (2006). Would you be happier if you were richer? A focusing illusion. *Science, 312*(5782), 1908–1910. doi: 10.1126/science.1129688

Landefeld, J. S., & McCulla, S. H. (2000). Accounting for nonmarket household production within a national accounts framework. *Review of Income and Wealth, 46*(3), 289–307. doi: 10.1111/j.1475-4991.2000.tb00844.x

Liddle, B. (2004). Demographic dynamics and per capita environmental impact: Using panel regressions and household decompositions to examine population and transport. *Population and Environment, 26*(1), 23–39. doi: 10.1023/B:POEN.0000039951.37276.f3

Liddle, B. (2014). Impact of population, age structure, and urbanization on carbon emissions/energy consumption: Evidence from macro-level, cross-country analyses. *Population and Environment, 35*(3), 286–304. doi: 10.1007/s11111-013-0198-4

Liu, J., Daily, G. C., Ehrlich, P. R., & Luck, G. W. (2003). Effects of household dynamics on resource consumption and biodiversity. *Nature, 421*, 530–533.

Lutzenhiser, L. (1993). Social and behavioral aspects of energy use. *Annual Review of Energy, 18*(1), 247–289.

Marszal-Pomianowska, A., Heiselberg, P., & Kalyanova Larsen, O. (2016). Household electricity demand profiles—A high-resolution load model to facilitate modelling of energy flexible buildings. *Energy, 103*, 487–501. doi: 10.1016/j.energy.2016.02.159

Michelson, W. H. (2015). *Time use: Expanding explanation in the social sciences*: Routledge.

Mishra, V., Smyth, R., & Sharma, S. (2009). The energy-GDP nexus: Evidence from a panel of Pacific Island countries. *Resource and Energy Economics, 31*(3), 210–220. doi: 10.1016/j.reseneeco.2009.04.002

Nair, G., Gustavsson, L., & Mahapatra, K. (2010). Factors influencing energy efficiency investments in existing Swedish residential buildings. *Energy Policy, 38*, 2956–2963.

National Bureau of Statistics. (2016). *Chinese energy statistical yearbook*: China Statistics Press.

National Bureau of Statistics. (2021). *Chinese energy statistical yearbook 2020*. Beijing, China: China Statistics Press.

Newman, P. W. G., & Kenworthy, J. R. (1996). The land use—transport connection: An overview. *Land Use Policy, 13*(1), 1–22. doi: 10.1016/0264-8377(95)00027-5

O'Neill, B. C., & Chen, B. S. (2002). Demographic determinants of household energy use in the United States. *Population and Development Review, 28*(Supplement: Population and Environment: Methods of Analysis), 53–88. Retrieved from http://www.jstor.org/stable/3115268

Ouyang, J., & Hokao, K. (2009). Energy-saving potential by improving occupants' behavior in urban residential sector in Hangzhou City, China. *Energy and Buildings, 41*(7), 711–720. doi: 10.1016/j.enbuild.2009.02.003

Permana, A. S., Abd Aziz, N., & Siong, H. C. (2015). Is mom energy efficient? A study of gender, household energy consumption and family decision making in Indonesia. *Energy Research & Social Science, 6*, 78–86. doi: 10.1016/j.erss.2014.12.007

Pollmann-Schult, M. (2017). Sons, daughters, and the parental division of paid work and housework. *Journal of Family Issues, 38*, 100–123.

Poortinga, W., Steg, L., Vlek, C., & Wiersma, G. (2003). Household preferences for energy-saving measures: A conjoint analysis. *Journal of Economic Psychology, 24*, 49–64.

Poumanyvong, P., & Kaneko, S. (2010). Does urbanization lead to less energy use and lower CO_2 emissions? A cross-country analysis. *Ecological Economics, 70*(2), 434–444. doi: 10.1016/j.ecolecon.2010.09.029

Ramírez-Mendiola, J. L., Grünewald, P., & Eyre, N. (2018). Linking intraday variations in residential electricity demand loads to consumers' activities: What's missing? *Energy and Buildings, 161*, 63–71. doi: 10.1016/j.enbuild.2017.12.012

Raty, R., & Carlsson-Kanyama, A. (2010). Energy consumption by gender in some European countries. *Energy Policy*, *38*(1), 646–649. doi: 10.1016/j.enpol.2009.08.010

Rau, H. (2015). Time use and resource consumption. In *International encyclopedia of the social & behavioral sciences* (pp. 373–378). doi: 10.1016/b978-0-08-097086-8.91090-0

Richardson, I., Thomson, M., Infield, D., & Clifford, C. (2010). Domestic electricity use: A high-resolution energy demand model. *Energy and Buildings*, *42*(10), 1878–1887. doi: 10.1016/j.enbuild.2010.05.023

Sanquist, T. F., Orr, H., Shui, B., & Bittner, A. C. (2012). Lifestyle factors in US residential electricity consumption. *Energy Policy*, *42*, 354–364.

Schipper, L., Bartlett, S., Hawk, D., & Vine, E. (1989). Linking life-styles and energy use: A matter of time? *Annual Review of Energy*, *14*, 273–320.

Schwanen, T., & Wang, D. (2014). Well-being, context, and everyday activities in space and time. *Annals of the Association of American Geographers*, *104*(4), 833–851. doi: 10.1080/00045608.2014.912549

Shahbaz, M., Loganathan, N., Muzaffar, A. T., Ahmed, K., & Ali Jabran, M. (2016). How urbanization affects CO_2 emissions in Malaysia? The application of STIRPAT model. *Renewable and Sustainable Energy Reviews*, *57*, 83–93. doi: 10.1016/j.rser.2015.12.096

Stern, P. C. (2000). Toward a coherent theory of environmentally significant behavior. *Journal of Social Issues*, *56*(3), 407–424. doi: 10.1111/0022-4537.00175

Stern, P. C., Dietz, T., & Kalof, L. (1993). Value orientations, gender, and environmental concern. *Environment and Behavior*, *25*(3), 322–348. doi: 10.1177/0013916593255002

Szalai, A. (1974). The use of time. Daily activities of urban and suburban populations in twelve countries. *The Economic Journal*, *84*(335), 691–694.

Tjørring, L., Jensen, C. L., Hansen, L. G., & Andersen, L. M. (2018). Increasing the flexibility of electricity consumption in private households: Does gender matter? *Energy Policy*, *118*, 9–18. doi: 10.1016/j.enpol.2018.03.006

Torriti, J. (2012). Demand side management for the European supergrid: Occupancy variances of European single-person households. *Energy Policy*, *44*, 199–206. doi: 10.1016/j.enpol.2012.01.039

Torriti, J. (2017). Understanding the timing of energy demand through time use data: Time of the day dependence of social practices. *Energy Research & Social Science*, *25*, 37–47. doi: 10.1016/j.erss.2016.12.004

UNFPA. (2016). *ICPD Beyond 2014 High-Level Global Commitments: Implementing the Population and Development Agenda (978-1-61800-880-0)*. Retrieved from

United Nations. (1996). *Beijing Declaration and Platform for Action: The Fourth World Conference on Women*. Beijing.

United Nations. (2015). *World Urbanization Prospects: The 2014 Revision*, (ST/ESA/SER.A/366). Retrieved from https://esa.un.org/unpd/wup/Publications/Files/WUP2014-Report.pdf

United Nations. (2016). *United Nations Statistics Division Time Use Data Portal*. Retrieved from unstats.un.org/unsd/gender/timeuse/index.html

United Nations. (2017a). *World Population Ageing*. New York.

United Nations. (2017b). *World Population Prospects: The 2017 Revision*. New York.

United Nations Department of Economic and Social Affairs. (2005). *Guide to Producing Statistics on Time Use Measuring Paid and Unpaid Work*. New York.

Van de Kaa, D. J. (1987). Europe's second demographic transition. *Population Bulletin, 42*, 1–59.

Wang, C., Wang, F., Zhang, X., Yang, Y., Su, Y., Ye, Y., & Zhang, H. (2017). Examining the driving factors of energy related carbon emissions using the extended STIRPAT model based on IPAT identity in Xinjiang. *Renewable and Sustainable Energy Reviews, 67*, 51–61. doi: 10.1016/j.rser.2016.09.006

Wang, P., Wu, W., Zhu, B., & Wei, Y. (2013). Examining the impact factors of energy-related CO_2 emissions using the STIRPAT model in Guangdong Province, China. *Applied Energy, 106*, 65–71. doi: 10.1016/j.apenergy.2013.01.036

Wang, Q., Wu, S., Zeng, Y., & Wu, B. (2016). Exploring the relationship between urbanization, energy consumption, and CO_2 emissions in different provinces of China. *Renewable and Sustainable Energy Reviews, 54*, 1563–1579. doi: 10.1016/j.rser.2015.10.090.

Wei, Y. M., Liu, L. C., Fan, Y., & Wu, G. (2007). The impact of lifestyle on energy use and CO_2 emission: An empirical analysis of China's residents. *Energy Policy, 35*(1), 247–257. doi: 10.1016/j.enpol.2005.11.020

Widén, J., & Wäckelgård, E. (2010). A high-resolution stochastic model of domestic activity patterns and electricity demand. *Applied Energy, 87*(6), 1880–1892. doi: 10.1016/j.apenergy.2009.11.006

Wiedenhofer, D., Smetschka, B., Akenji, L., Jalas, M., & Haberl, H. (2018). Household time use, carbon footprints, and urban form: A review of the potential contributions of everyday living to the 1.5°C climate target. *Current Opinion in Environmental Sustainability, 30*, 7–17. doi: 10.1016/j.cosust.2018.02.007

Xu, B., & Lin, B. (2015). How industrialization and urbanization process impacts on CO_2 emissions in China: Evidence from nonparametric additive regression models. *Energy Economics, 48*, 188–202. doi: 10.1016/j.eneco.2015.01.005

Xu, Y., Song, J., & Zhang, W. (2014). Decomposing the impacts of time use on energy consumption. *Energy Procedia, 61*, 1888–1892.

York, R. (2003). Cross-national variation in the size of passenger car fleets: A study in environmentally significant consumption. *Population and Environment, 25*, 119–140.

Yu, B., Wei, Y., Kei, G., & Matsuoka, Y. (2018). Future scenarios for energy consumption and carbon emissions due to demographic transitions in Chinese households. *Nature Energy, 3*(2), 109–118. doi: 10.1038/s41560-017-0053-4

Zha, D., Zhou, D., & Zhou, P. (2010). Driving forces of residential CO_2 emissions in urban and rural China: An index decomposition analysis. *Energy Policy*, *38*(7), 3377–3383.

Zhang, C., & Lin, Y. (2012). Panel estimation for urbanization, energy consumption and CO_2 emissions: A regional analysis in China. *Energy Policy*, *49*, 488–498.

Zhao, X., Li, N., & Ma, C. (2012). Residential energy consumption in urban China: A decomposition analysis. *Energy Policy*, *41*, 644–653. doi: 10.1016/j.enpol.2011.11.027

Zheng, X., Wei, C., Qin, P., Guo, J., Yu, Y., Song, F., & Chen, Z. (2014). Characteristics of residential energy consumption in China: Findings from a household survey. *Energy Policy*, *75*, 126–135. doi: 10.1016/j.enpol.2014.07.016

Zhou, H., Li, Z., Xue, D., & Lei, Y. (2010). Time use patterns between maintenance, subsistence and leisure activities: A case study in China. *Social Indicators Research*, *105*(1), 121–136. doi: 10.1007/s11205-010-9768-3

Zhou, N., Fridley, D., Khanna, N. Z., Ke, J., McNeil, M., & Levine, M. (2013). China's energy and emissions outlook to 2050: Perspectives from bottom-up energy end-use model. *Energy Policy*, *53*, 51–62. doi: 10.1016/j.enpol.2012.09.065

2   Time use in evolving China

2.1 The Chinese time-use survey (CTUS)

In China, time-use survey has been developed into a regular stand-alone national survey at a steady pace. Earliest efforts could be traced back to 2001 when the "Outline for the Development of Chinese Women (2001–2010)" was launched. From then on, the National Bureau of Statistics has engaged actively in the research and development of the Chinese Time-Use Survey. Personnel and resources have been assigned to the investigation of surveys previously conducted in the international standards like International Time-Use Survey, American Time-Use Survey, and Harmonized European Time-Use Surveys. Between 2003 and 2007, a cooperative project on time-use surveys with Statistics Sweden, the country with the longest history of time-use study, was launched to gain first-hand knowledge and experience. In 2005, a pilot survey was conducted in Zhejiang and Yunnan provinces. And finally in 2008 and 2018, the first and second national time-use surveys were implemented (National Bureau of Statistics, 2009, 2019).

Both rounds of Chinese Time-Use Survey (CTUS) were administrated by the National Bureau of Statistics of China. The social science division designed the survey instruments, and investigation forces at the provincial and city/county level carried out the on-site data collection. Survey setting, such as sample sizes, regions, and periods were kept highly identical to enhance the comparability of results. They were both conducted in May, covered ten provinces (Heilongjiang, Beijing, Hebei, Zhenjiang, Anhui, Henan, Guangdong, Sichuan, Yunnan, and Gansu, as illustrated in Figure 2.1), and sampled around 60,000 individuals aged between 15 and 74 from 20,000 households. Sampled households were drawn from the Chinese Household Survey

DOI: 10.4324/9780429291708-2

Figure 2.1 Ten Chinese provinces sampled in the 2008 and 2018 time-use
          surveys.

(National Bureau of Statistics, 2009, 2019).

in the previous year in three-stage stratification sampling with respect
to regions, population, and income level (National Bureau of Statistics,
2009, 2019).

Questionnaires in the CTUSs were designed under international
standards. They consist of three sections—time-use diary, post-diary
questions, and household information—to record respondents' time-
use pattern and relevant contextual information. The diaries are time-
sequenced tables that allow respondents to record all activities
undertaken in a day from 4:00 am on a reference day to 4:00 am of the
following day chronologically, at intervals of ten minutes in the 2008
CTUS and at 15 minutes in the 2018 version (See the translated 2008
CTUS and 2018 CTUS in Appendices I and II towards the end of this
chapter). Activity information is collected in each activity entry, which
include primary activity, secondary activity, location or transport, and
other participate (s) on 2008; and primary activity, internet usage and
other participate(s) on 2018. In both rounds, respondents are requested
to complete diaries for two days, one weekday (Monday to Friday) and
one weekend day (Saturday & Sunday). Post-diary questions are

general questions to ensure data quality of the diary, such as working nature of the reference day, and time of diary competition. Finally, demographic information of all household members, including gender, age, education level, income level, and relation to the household holder, are collected from the household holder in the sector of household information. And there was not much changes between two surveys (National Bureau of Statistics, 2009, 2019).

Activity categorizations in time-use diary and related data processing procedures, in contrast, differed considerably between 2008 and 2018 CTUS and changed from post-coded full-time diary to precoded light-time diary. In the former survey, the diary was designed with open-ended questions for primary and secondary activities. Respondents were allowed to describe the activities in their own words; and their verbal answers were later converted into standardized numeric codes by officers for further statistical analyses. In 2018, it was changed to a pre-coded system instead. Respondents needed to choose from the pre-defined list of activity categories to describe their primary pre-coded activities (National Bureau of Statistics, 2019). Such a change would enhance the efficiency and reduce the cost of data collection and processing. However, it has caused significant losses of activity details. Activity classification scheme have downsized from 113 third tier, 61 second-tier and nine first-tier activity categories in 2008 to only 20 second-tier and six first-tier categories in 2018 (See activity classification scheme in Appendices I and II).

The descriptive statistics of the respondents' demographic distribution are given in Table 2.1. The samples contains respondents of different residences (urban/rural), genders, ages, education levels, income levels, and provinces; and the distributions have been slightly varied between 2008 and 2018. Samples of both years were approximately equally divided between men and women and between urban and rural residents, with slightly growing shares of urban residents and women. The median education attainments were both at junior secondary school, but the distibution in 2018 became more polarized with increasing shares in both ends. More obvious changes within these ten years were spotted at ages and income levels. Sampled respondents were significantly older and richer. The median age increased by ten years to 45–54 years-old; and the share of those aged 55 or older also rose by 12.1%. The median income level has even more than doubled from RMB500–1000 to RMB2000–5000. Finally in the geographical distribution, sampled respondents were relatively evenly distributed, except the sampled population in Sichuan in 2008 that only accounted for 4.9%.

Table 2.1 Demographic distribution of respondents sampled in 2008 and 2018 CTUS (National Bureau of Statistics, 2009, 2019).

Variables	2008	2018	Variables	2008	2018
			Monthly income (RMB)		
Residence (%)	%	%		%	%
Urban	52.83	60.84	No income	14.87	15.10
Rural	47.17	39.16	<500	19.44	7.08
Gender (%)			500–1,000	26.57	7.94
Male	49.04	48.53	1,000–2,000	25.76	17.03
Female	50.96	51.47	2,000–5,000	12	40.84
Age (%)			5,000–10,000	1.00	10.02
15–24	10.04	7.62	>10,000	0.15	2.00
25–34	15.08	14.37	Province (%)		
35–44	27.75	18.36	Beijing	10.05	8.72
45–54	24.83	25.26	Hebei	12.86	10.48
55–64	16.09	18.84	Heilongjiang	9.99	8.03
65–74	6.21	15.56	Zhejiang	8.88	10.83
Education Attainment (%)			Anhui	12.33	8.58
Never educated	4.38	4.95	Henan	13.47	12.28
Primary	16.83	19.28	Guangdong	8.86	13.56
Junior Secondary	34.73	36.40	Sichuan	4.94	11.51
Senior Secondary	25.37	19.45	Yunnan	9.18	8.81
University or above	18.70	19.92	Gansu	9.45	7.20

We got official approval to utilize the microdata of the 2008 Chinese Time-Use Survey from the Social Science Divison of the National Bureau of Statistics. Although the 2018 microdata have not been made available to us, detailed statistics data were published to allow in-depth analysis and longititudinal comparison (National Bureau of Statistics, 2019). As shown in Table 2.2, this set of microdata consists of six files: *personal information file* recording respondents' demographic and economic characteristics; two *diary episode files* documenting information of all activities undertaken on a sampled weekday and weekend day; and three *aggregate files* summarizing the amount of time spent on a particular activity by each respondent based on the third-tier activity categorization system. In this research, time spent on each activity and

Table 2.2 Variables lists of Personal Information and Diary Episode (National Bureau of Statistics, 2009).

Personal Information	Diary Episode
Province (Municipality)	Province (Municipality)
County (District, City)	County (District, City)
Household ID	Household ID
Person ID	Person ID
Distance from home to workplace/ school	Primary Activity
Monthly Income	Activity Location/Transport mode
Relation to Householder	Secondary Activity
Gender	Activity Duration
Year of Birth	Activity Timeslots
Month of Birth	With whom
Ethics	Activity
Education Attainment	Weekday or Weekend/holidays
Marital Status	
Occupation	
Age	
Urban/Rural	

number of users sharing an appliance during an activity are reestimated with regard to our refined activity categorization by processing three data files, *personal information, diary episode (Weekday)*, and *diary episode (Weekend)*.

Activity categories presented in this sector is harmonised to enable the comparison between 2008 and 2018 CTUS (Table 2.3).

2.2 Time-use-defined lifestyles in China

Various time-use-defined lifestyles could be clearly distinguished as people with different socio-economic features allocate significantly different amounts of time to various daily activities. The 2008 and 2018 time-use surveys will be examined to sketch the evolution of these lifestyles with China's rapid social changes together with economic development.

The lifestyles refer to typical Chinese residents on typical days, or averages to represent groups in focus for comparing across groups and

Table 2.3 Activity categorization in this study and related categories in 2008 and 2018 CTUS (National Bureau of Statistics, 2009, 2019)

Activity Description	2008 (Second-Tier Code)	2018 (Second-Tier Code)
Personal care and maintenance	Personal Hygiene (03); Religious activities (04); Smoking (05); Other personal care activities (06)	Personal hygiene (52); Medical Service (54)
Sleeping	Sleep (01)	Sleep (51)
Paid Work	Formal employment (11–12); Household Primary Production (21–25); Household Secondary Production and Construction (31–38); Household Service Production (41-47)	Formal employment (11); Household Production (12)
Unpaid Work	Unpaid Domestic Work (51–58); Caring for household members and others (61–65)	Housework (21); Child care (22); Elderly care (23); Grocery purchase (24); Voluntary activity (25)
Study	Study (71–75)	Study (31)
Meal	Meal (02)	Food & Drink (53)
Leisure and Socializing	Reading (81); Sports (82); Hobbies, games, and leisure activities (83); Attending cultural, entertainment, and sports events (84); Socializing (85)	Fitness (41); Listen ratio/music (42); Reading (44); Leisure & entertainment (45); Socializing (46)
Watching TV	Watching TV (814)[1]	Watch TV (43)
Transportation	All Travels (09; 19; 29; 39; 49; 59; 69; 79; 89)	Transportation (61)

1 Note: Watching TV (814) was a third-tier activity code in 2008 CTUS.

analysing the longitudinal and demographic differences in between (Gravetter & Wallnau, 2016). The concept of typical individual is quite commonly used in energy- and time-use studies. In energy studies, particularly those taking micro-level approaches, the weighted mean is often used to represent a typical individual of a specific group in evaluating its energy consumption and environmental consequences

(Tso, 2003; Zheng et al., 2014). It has also been used in behavioral energy studies to characterize household and appliances characteristics in modeling energy load curves (Chiou, 2009; Yao, Chen, & Li, 2012). For time-use studies, *it often refers to typical day of a typical individual* (Robinson & Martin, 2011). Using the American Time-Use Survey as an example, their results often published in per person per day, describing how much time a typical American spends on various daily activities on a typical day. This approach of result reporting is shared by other time-use surveys like Harmonized European Time-Use Survey and the Chinese Time-Use Survey (SEPA, 2006).

- **Weekday and weekend/holiday lifestyles**

Like most people in the world, the Chinese adults have very different lifestyles on weekdays and weekends/holidays (Figures 2.2 and 2.3). In 2018, an average Chinese spent 290 minutes on a weekday for paid work, 150 minutes for unpaid work, 97 minutes to watch TV, 124 minutes for other leisure and socializing, and 40 minutes in transport. On a weekend/holiday, the corresponding time use became 198 minutes, 180 minutes, 110 minutes, 164 minutes and 32 minutes, respectively.

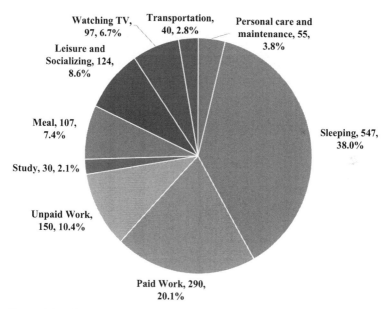

Figure 2.2 Lifestyle in a typical weekday in 2018 by daily time use (minutes).
(National Bureau of Statistics, 2019).

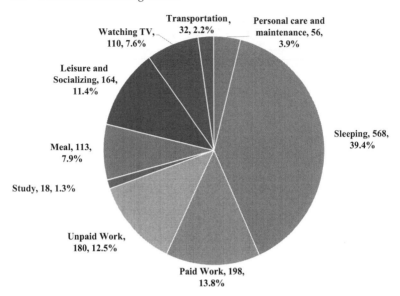

Figure 2.3 Lifestyle in a typical weekend/holiday in 2018 by daily time use (minutes).

(National Bureau of Statistics, 2019).

In other words, people worked much less for their jobs, did more household chores and enjoyed more leisure activities on weekends/holidays (Figure 2.4). The difference was largely similar to that in 2008, indicating that the two lifestyles are generally stable through the years.

From 2008 to 2018, the average Chinese lifestyle evolved significantly, and the changes were similar between weekdays and weekends/holidays (Figure 2.4). On a typical day, while an average Chinese adult watched TV for 26 fewer minutes, 41 more minutes were spent for other leisure and socializing. A big difference in the decade and a probable cause of the time-use changes were the sharp rise of Internet usage due to greater coverage and more convenient access through, most notably, the widespread use of smart phones and 4G network. Even to watch television programs, due to the convenience and instant availability, people might also choose online television watching on those devices, instead of television itself (Wang, Ding, Lu, & Gu, 2012). In addition, over the decade they were occupied six minutes less for paid work but ten minutes more for unpaid work. The biggest change happened for transportation from 78 minutes in 2008 to just

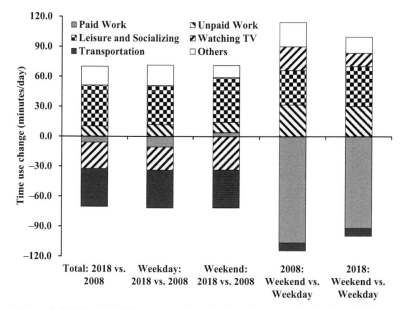

Figure 2.4 Lifestyle differences and evolution between the 2008 and 2018 time-use surveys.

(National Bureau of Statistics, 2009, 2019).

38 minutes in 2018. This might correspond to the improvement in China's transportation system. Total length of paved road increased from 3.7 to 4.8 million kms, and those of railway increased from 79 to 132 thousand kms. The private car ownership skyrocketed from 26.4 to 147.5 private cars/1,000 people (National Bureau of Statistics of China, 2020).

• **Urban and rural lifestyles**

China has long been featured by a significant, multi-faceted urban-rural gap. In 2018, a typical urban Chinese adult spent 240 minutes in paid work, 163 minutes in unpaid work, 99 minutes in watching TV, 152 minutes in other leisure and socializing, and 43 minutes in transport (Figure 2.5). The corresponding time use for a typical rural Chinese adult was 301 minutes, 155 minutes, 105 minutes, 107 minutes and 30 minutes, respectively (Figure 2.6). The most important difference between the two lifestyles was that rural people tended to engage much more time in paid work, being 62 minutes longer. It could reflect the more demanding nature of a primary sector job.

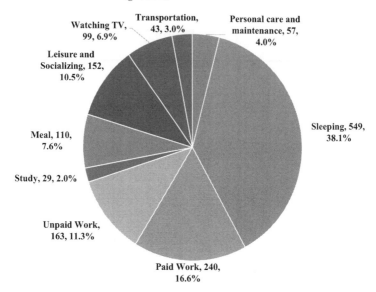

Figure 2.5 Lifestyle of a typical urban Chinese in 2018 by daily time use (minutes).

(National Bureau of Statistics, 2019).

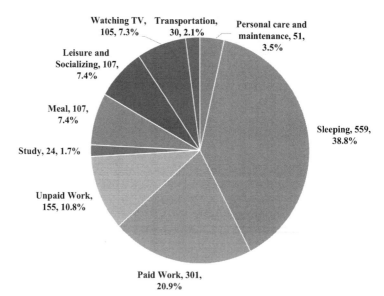

Figure 2.6 Lifestyle of a typical rural Chinese in 2018 by daily time use (minutes).

(National Bureau of Statistics, 2019).

The urban-rural gap in 2018, although still significant, was much smaller than that in 2008 when paid work occupied 132 more minutes in a rural adult's daily routine (Figure 2.7). The cause was rooted in both urban and rural evolution as an urban adult worked longer and a rural adult worked less (Figure 2.7). Rural Chinese were less engaged in time-intensive, but low financially-rewarding agriculture, and more in industrial and commercial jobs (National Bureau of Statistics, 2020). The most significant change took place in urban China over weekends/holidays when 57 more minutes were allocated to paid work (Figure 2.8). It might reflect China's recent workaholic culture such as the infamous "996" in the tech industry (work from 9:00 am to 9:00 pm, six days a week). As a result, weekends/holidays in urban China differed from weekdays to a significantly less extent. In comparison, rural China did not witness such a phenomenon (Figure 2.9).

Because every day has exactly 24 hours, the urban-rural gap was also narrowed from other time-use activities after the shrinking difference in paid work. Both urban and rural Chinese spent more time in leisure and socializing, but the rural increase was 20 minutes greater (Figure 2.7). Overall, the urban and rural lifestyles in China were

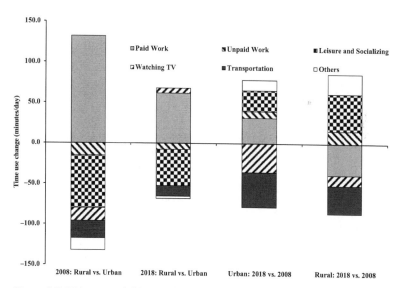

Figure 2.7 Urban-rural lifestyle differences and evolution between the 2008 and 2018 time-use surveys.

(National Bureau of Statistics, 2009, 2019).

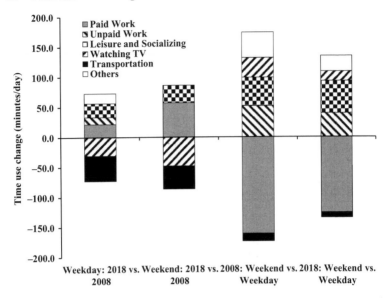

Figure 2.8 Urban lifestyle differences and evolution between the 2008 and 2018 time-use surveys.

(National Bureau of Statistics, 2009, 2019).

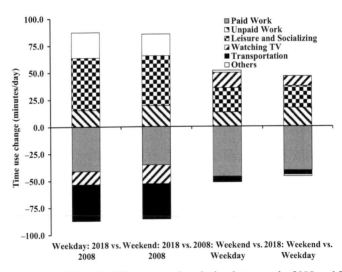

Figure 2.9 Rural lifestyle differences and evolution between the 2008 and 2018 time-use surveys.

(National Bureau of Statistics, 2009, 2019).

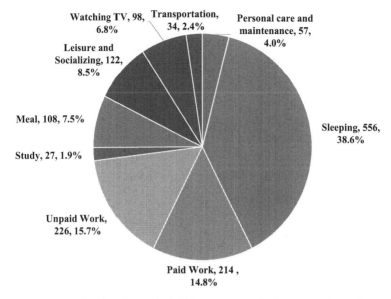

Figure 2.10 Lifestyle of a typical Chinese woman in 2018 by daily time use (minutes).

(National Bureau of Statistics, 2019).

rapidly converging as indicated by their time-use patterns, mainly with the urbanization of rural lifestyles with less work and more leisure.

• **Gendered lifestyles**

Lifestyle is highly gendered. In 2018, a typical Chinese woman did 226 minutes of unpaid work, more than the 214 minutes of paid work on an average day (Figure 2.10). In comparison, a typical Chinese man spent much more time in paid work (316 minutes) than in unpaid work (90 minutes) (Figure 2.11). This contrast accounted for most of the differences in the gendered lifestyles. The traditional gender gap remained deep and became even wider from 2008 to 2018 (Figure 2.12). Men are breadwinners and women take care of the household. After the decade, women were engaged 17 minutes less in paid work, while men took five more minutes (Figure 2.12). The widening gap was mainly caused by women's less paid work on weekdays and men's more paid work on weekends/holidays (Figures 2.13 and 2.14).

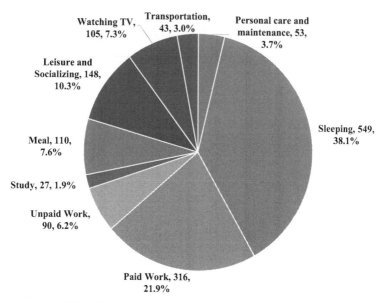

Figure 2.11 Lifestyle of a typical Chinese man in 2018 by daily time use (minutes).

(National Bureau of Statistics, 2019).

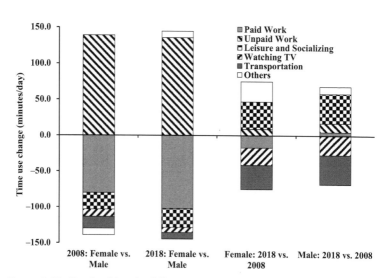

Figure 2.12 Gender lifestyle differences and evolution between the 2008 and 2018 time-use surveys.

(National Bureau of Statistics, 2009, 2019).

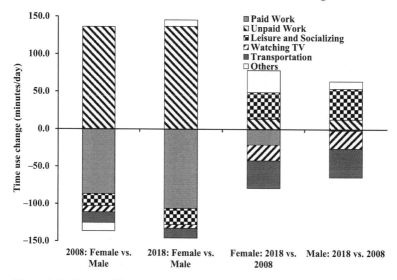

Figure 2.13 Gender lifestyle differences and evolution on weekdays between the 2008 and 2018 time-use surveys.

(National Bureau of Statistics, 2009, 2019).

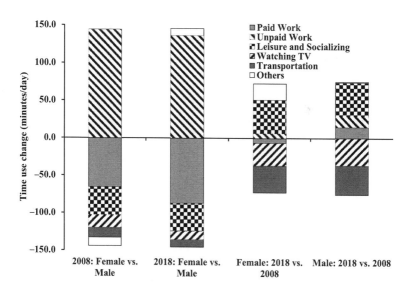

Figure 2.14 Gender lifestyle differences and evolution on weekends/holidays between the 2008 and 2018 time-use surveys.

(National Bureau of Statistics, 2009, 2019).

The gendered lifestyle gap was also reflected in leisure activities. As women spent more than in work (440 minutes in 2018) than men did (406 minutes), they had less time for watching TV (five minutes fewer) and leisure and socializing (22 minutes fewer) (Figure 2.12). Furthermore, women were consistently much less mobile than men (17 minutes fewer in 2008 and 11 minutes fewer in 2018), while both genders used less time for transportation. The gender gap was about equally wide between weekdays and weekends/holidays. In other words, the gender roles were not weakened on those days when men were less engaged in breadwinning.

- **Life stage and lifestyles**

Individual lifestyles evolve significantly corresponding to life stages. Although the Chinese Time-Use Survey only targets adults above 15 years old, three clear life stages could be distinguished. In comparison with the average lifestyle in 2018, those young Chinese in the age group 15–24 were 116 minutes less occupied in paid work, 109 minutes less in unpaid work, and 58 minutes less in watching TV, while the saved time was mostly used for study, being 272 minutes more (Figure 2.15). Their lifestyle indicates that most of them were still

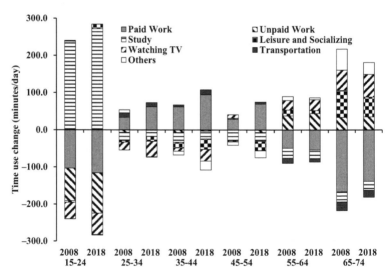

Figure 2.15 Lifestyle variations by age between the 2008 and 2018 time-use surveys (difference in minutes with the year's overall average).

(National Bureau of Statistics, 2009, 2019).

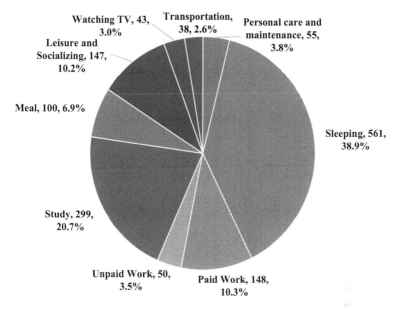

Figure 2.16 Lifestyle of a typical Chinese in youth age (15–24 years old) in 2018 by daily time use (minutes).

(National Bureau of Statistics, 2019).

studying in high school or university as the time for study more than doubled that for paid work in 2018 (Figure 2.16). This youth, study-dominated lifestyle was even more clearly distinguished in 2018 than in 2008 as 31 more minutes were allocated for study (Figure 2.19). It should have reflected the trend that more Chinese are receiving more years of education, especially in universities.

Those Chinese in the primary working age (25–54 years old) allocated significantly more time to paid work and less time for leisure activities. In 2018, they worked for 339 minutes on an average day, spent 76 minutes in watching TV and 113 minutes for leisure and socializing (Figure 2.17). Those in early retirement age (65–74 years old) had much less time for paid work and more for leisure activities (Figure 2.15). Nevertheless, they did significantly more unpaid work, 194 minutes in 2018 (Figure 2.18).

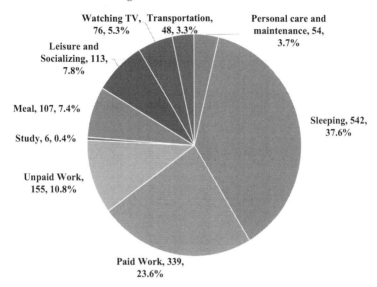

Figure 2.17 Lifestyle of a typical Chinese in prime working age (25–54 years old) in 2018 by daily time use (minutes).

(National Bureau of Statistics, 2019).

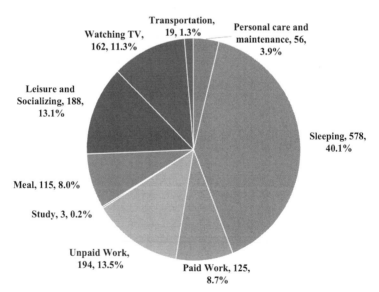

Figure 2.18 Lifestyle of a typical Chinese senior citizen in retirement age (65–74 years old) in 2018 by daily time use (minutes).

(National Bureau of Statistics, 2019).

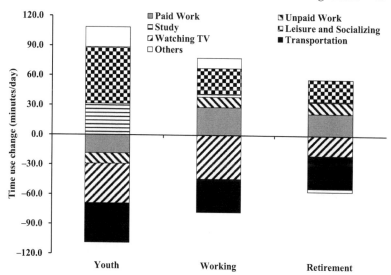

Figure 2.19 Lifestyle evolution (2018 vs 2008) between the two time-use surveys.

(National Bureau of Statistics, 2009, 2019).

Among the three life stage lifestyles, the youth lifestyle changed the most from 2008 to 2018 with a swing of 109 minutes (Figure 2.19). All three groups spent less time for transportation and watching TV, and more time in Leisure and Socializing. It could imply that although China's Internet coverage was a factor to change young people's lifestyle, it also exerted significant, despite smaller, impacts on the working and retirement lifestyles.

• **Education and lifestyles**

Education plays a crucial role in shaping the lifestyle of individuals. In 2018, those Chinese adults who received no schooling were much less occupied in paid work than the average, being 104 minutes fewer (Figure 2.20). The change was especially startling in comparison with the difference in 2008, when this group worked 11 minutes more than the average. In contrast, those with university education and above tended to work more in paid jobs in 2018 and less in 2008. These two lifestyles were distinctly different. In 2018, the latter group spent 274 minutes in paid work, while the former group only used 160 minutes (Figures 2.21 and 2.22). Even their leisure time use had very different

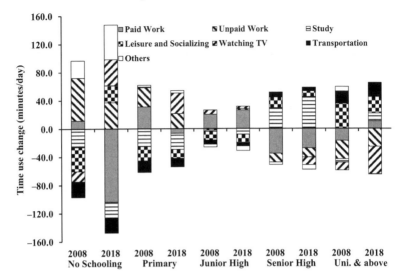

Figure 2.20 Lifestyle variations by education level between the 2008 and 2018 time-use surveys (difference in minutes with the year's overall average; for the University & above category, the 2018 survey differentiated programs for associate degrees, bachelor's degrees, and postgraduate degrees, while the 2008 survey had only one overall category. For purposes of comparability, the 2018 data refer to those in the bachelor's degree programmes.)

(National Bureau of Statistics, 2009, 2019).

structures. The former group allocated 138 minutes in watching TV in 2018, while the latter group only got 62 minutes. It could reflect that the penetration of the Internet could be highly correlated with education levels. Those without schooling may be the slowest in keeping pace with the Internet era.

From 2008 to 2018, those without schooling had the most significant lifestyle changes (Figure 2.23). Generally speaking, the more educated a Chinese citizen was, the more paid work would be done. These may correspond to the transformation of China's economy over the years from labour-intensive toward more knowledge based. Low-skilled jobs in China could be relocated to other overseas economies with lower wages. Those without schooling and inadequate education may thus have been encountering serious unemployment to significantly reflect and affect China's social changes.

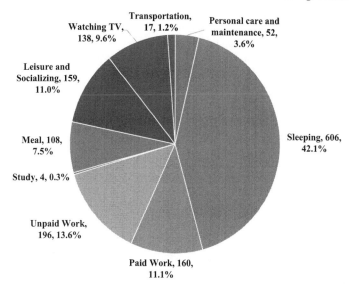

Figure 2.21 Lifestyle of a typical Chinese with no schooling in 2018 by daily time use (minutes).

(National Bureau of Statistics, 2019).

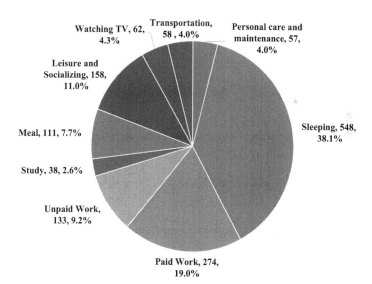

Figure 2.22 Lifestyle of a typical Chinese with university education or above in 2018 by daily time use (minutes).

(National Bureau of Statistics, 2019).

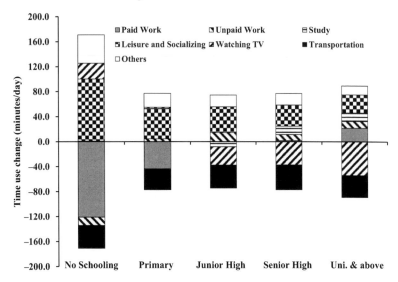

Figure 2.23 Lifestyle evolution (2018 vs 2008) by education level between the two time-use surveys.

(National Bureau of Statistics, 2009, 2019).

- **Income and lifestyles**

Income and lifestyles are highly correlated. More time in paid work tended to result in higher income, while those with higher income also worked more. Those without income were mostly students and house-wives as their study time was 122 minutes more than the average and 69 minutes more for unpaid work in 2018 (Figure 2.24). Although in 2008, those with higher income had more time for leisure and trans-portation, the time-use pattern changed significantly in 2018 when they spent more time mainly in paid work (Figure 2.24).

Low- and high-income people lead very different lifestyles. For those with a monthly income between 500 and 1,000 RMB, a typical day in 2018 featured 265 minutes of paid work, 182 minutes of unpaid work, 124 minutes in watching TV, 118 minutes in leisure and social-izing, and 24 minutes for transportation (Figure 2.25). In contrast, those who earned more than 10,000 RMB/month did more paid work (345 minutes) but less unpaid work (102 minutes). They watched much less TV (66 minutes) but got more time for leisure and socializing

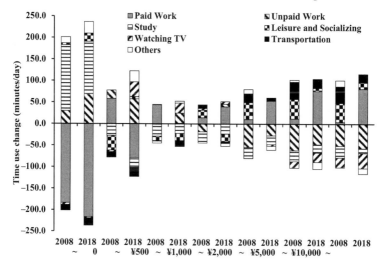

Figure 2.24 Lifestyle variations by monthly income level between the 2008 and 2018 time-use surveys (difference in minutes with the year's overall average).

(National Bureau of Statistics, 2009, 2019).

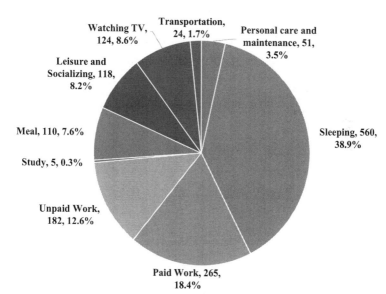

Figure 2.25 Lifestyle of a typical Chinese with low income (500–1000 RMB/month/person) in 2018 by daily time use (minutes).

(National Bureau of Statistics, 2019).

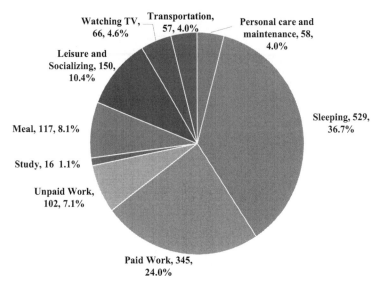

Figure 2.26   Lifestyle of a typical Chinese with high income (more than 10,000 RMB/month/person) in 2018 by daily time use (minutes).

(National Bureau of Statistics, 2019).

(150 minutes). They were also much more mobile with 57 minutes for transportation.

Over the decade from 2008 to 2018, family division of labor seemed to have deepened significantly as reflected in the time use for paid work. High-income Chinese worked a lot more and low-income ones saw even a large net reduction: 71 minutes more for those earning more than 10,000 RMB/month, and 48 minutes less for those earning between 500 and 1,000 RMB/month (Figure 2.27). Transportation occupied consistently less time for people at all income levels (Figure 2.26).

- **Spatial lifestyles: in-residence or absent from residence**

The location of activities is also a factor that should not be overlooked when we study time-use patterns and their impacts on residential energy consumption and CO_2 emissions. Often the more time a person spends in her/his residence, the more frequent she/he uses the electric

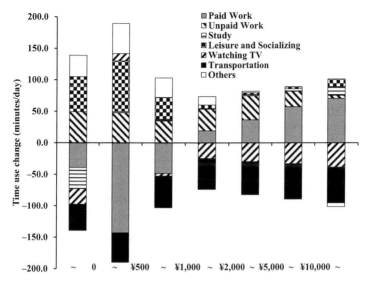

Figure 2.27 Lifestyle evolution (2018 vs 2008) by monthly income levels between the two time-use surveys.

(National Bureau of Statistics, 2009, 2019).

appliances in the home, resulting in higher residential electricity consumption and CO_2 emissions. In 2008, Chinese spent in average 1000.9 minutes (67.7%) per day at their own residences. As expected, sleeping occupied 527 minutes, being the most time-spending activity at home. Watching TV and unpaid work came second and third, with 119 minutes and 107 minutes, respectively. Paid work and study accounted for the least (Figure 2.28). Except paid work and study, other daily activities were mostly conducted in-residence.

Between weekdays and weekends/holidays, there was not much difference, except for paid work and study (Figure 2.29). The percentage of Chinese working and studying at home on weekdays is 13.0% higher than on weekends, indicating a stressful lifestyle that requires taking extra work and homework home to complete on weekdays. Some small differences (within 5%) could also be found, in that the proportion of time spent eating, relaxing, and watching TV at home was higher on weekends/holidays, while the proportion of time spent on unpaid work at home was higher on weekdays.

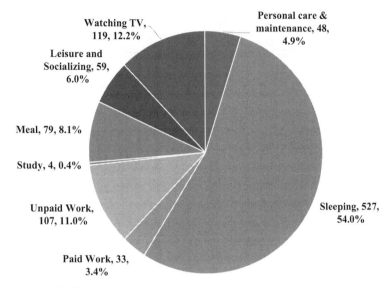

Figure 2.28 Share of in-residence activities in 2008 by daily time use (minutes). (National Bureau of Statistics, 2009).

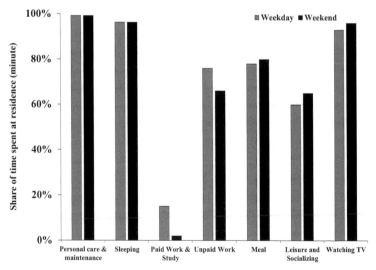

Figure 2.29 Share of time spent at respondent's residence in 2008 time-use survey by activity and day of the week.

(National Bureau of Statistics, 2009).

Appendix I The 2008 Chinese time-use survey

Time-use diary

Date of the Diary: 1 05 1 2008 (Day of the Week)

Timeslot	What are you doing? [Please describe primary activity undertaken and describe in detail]	When did the activity taken place? [Please selecte from the following location codes. If it is a transport activity, please select from transport code instead]	What activity did you also perform? [Please describe secondary activity performed simultaneously with the primary activity in detail]	Who was present at beginning of the primary activity?				
				Alone/ with Stranger	Family Members	Age 0–6	Age 7–64	Age ≥65	Other friend/ relative
4:00–4:10								
4:10–4:20								
......								
......								
The following day								
3:50–4:00								

Activity Location:

1. Home (Including others' home);
2. Workplace/School;
3. Street, Park, or other public area;
4. Bank, School, Post office, hotel, or services place;
5. Restaurant, Bar, or other catering place; 6.
6. Cinema, Karaoke, Sportsground, or other entertaining facility;
7. Other

Transport:

8. Walking;
9. Riding Bicycle/Motorcycle;
10. Public Transport;
11. Private Car;
12. Other motorized transport mode;
13. Animal Transport;
14. Other Transport

Activity classification

1st Tier	2nd Tier	3rd Tier	Descriptive
0			**Personal care and Maintenance**
	01		*Sleeping*
		011	Night sleep/essential sleep
		012	Incidental sleep/naps
		013	Sleep in sick
	02		*Meal*
		021	Eating a meal
		022	Drinking other than with meal or snack
		023	Eating a snack
	03		*Personal Hygiene*
		031	Personal/private hygiene activities
		032	Showering/bathing

(*Continued*)

Continued

1st Tier	2nd Tier	3rd Tier	Descriptive
		033	Grooming
		034	Other personal hygiene activities
	04	040	Religious activities
	05	050	Smoking
	06	060	Other personal care activities
	09	090	Travel related to personal care activities
1			**Formal Employment**
	11	111	Work, main work
		112	Work, part work
		113	Apprenticeship or internship
		114	Short breaks and interruption from work
		115	Training and studies related to work
		116	Looking for work
		117	Looking for/setting up business
	12	120	Other work-related activities
	19	199	Travel for work-related activities
2			**Household Primary Production**
	21	210	Growing of crops
	22	220	Growing of trees
	23	230	Farming of animals
	24	240	Fishing and aquatic farming
	25	250	Other household primary productive activities
	29	299	Travel related to household primary productive activities
3			**Household Secondary Production and Construction**
	31	310	Processing of agricultural products
	32	320	Processing of food products
	33	330	Making beverages
	34	340	Making textile, leather, and associated products

(*Continued*)

Continued

1st Tier	2nd Tier	3rd Tier	Descriptive
	35	350	Crafting-making using nonmetal materials
	36	360	Other household secondary productive activities
	37	370	Household construction activities
	38	380	Other household construction activities
	39	399	Travel related to household construction activities
4			**Household Service Production**
	41	410	Food vending and trading
	42	420	Providing repair, installation, and maintenance services
	43	430	Providing professional services
	44	440	Providing personal care services
	45	450	Transporting goods and passengers
	46	460	Paid domestic services
	47	470	Other household tertiary productive activities
	49	499	Travel related to household tertiary productive activities
5			**Unpaid Domestic Work**
	51		*Food preparation and cleaning*
		511	Preparing and serving food
		512	Cleaning up after a meal
	52		*Cleaning*
		521	Indoor cleaning
		522	Outdoor cleaning
	53		Laundry
		531	Washing clothes
		532	Drying, ironing, and storing clothes
		533	Mending and care of clothes

(*Continued*)

Continued

1st Tier	2nd Tier	3rd Tier	Descriptive
	54		*Purchasing for goods and services*
		541	Shopping for durable goods
		542	Window shopping
		543	Availing of repairing and maintenance services
		544	Shopping for administrative services
	55		*Pet care*
		551	Daily pet care
		552	Taking pets for veterinary care
		553	Care of grade
	56		*Household decoration, maintenance, and repair of dwellings*
		561	Household decoration, maintenance, and repairing
		562	Installation, servicing, and repair of household goods
		563	Vehicle maintenance and minor repairs
	57	570	Household management
	58	580	Other domestic work-related activities
	59	599	Travel related to domestic work
6			*Caring for household members and others*
	61		*Caring for children*
		611	Caring for children/physical care
		612	Teaching, training, helping children
		613	Minding children (passive care)
		614	Accompanying children to places
	62		*Caring for adults*
		621	Caring for adults/physical care
		622	Giving medical/healthcare to adults
		623	Accompanying adults to places

(*Continued*)

Continued

1st Tier	2nd Tier	3rd Tier	Descriptive
	63	630	Unpaid help to other households
	64	640	Community-organized services
	65	650	Other unpaid help to others
	69	699	Travel related to unpaid help to others
7			*Study*
	71		*General education*
		711	Attending classes and lectures
		712	Breaks/waiting at place of general education
		713	Self-study for distance education course work
	72		*Homework, course review, research*
		721	Homework, course review, research, and activities
	73	730	Additional study, nonformal education
	74	740	Career/professional development training and studies
	75	750	Other study-related activities
	79	799	Travel related to study-related activities
8			*Leisure and Socializing*
	81		*Reading*
		811	Reading books
		812	Reading periods
		813	Reading other specific materials
		814	Watching television
		815	Watching/listening to video programmes
		816	Listening to radio
		817	Listening to other audio media
		818	Using computer technology for reading or audio
		819	Surfing the Internet

(*Continued*)

Continued

1st Tier	2nd Tier	3rd Tier	Descriptive
	82		*Sports*
		821	Walking and running
		822	Martial art
		823	Aerobics, yoga, weight-training, and other fitness programmes
		824	Ball games
		825	Water sports
		826	Other sports
	83		*Hobbies, games and leisure activities*
		831	Card games, board games
		832	Computer games
		833	Social/group games
		834	Purchasing for collection
		835	Performing arts
	84		*Attending cultural, entertainment, and sports events*
		841	Attendance at movies
		842	Core activities: time spent attending cultural, entertainment and sports events, attendance at organized/mass cultural events
		843	Attendance at shows
		844	Attendance at sports events
	85		*Socializing*
		851	Talking, conversing
		852	Reading and writing mail
		853	Other socializing activities
	86	860	Other leisure activities
	89	899	Travel related to leisure activities
9	90	900	Unspecific time use

Appendix II The 2018 Chinese time-use survey

Time-use diary

Date of the Diary: / 05 / 2018 (Day of the Week)

(Time)	4	15	30	45	5	15	30	45	6	15	30	45	7	15	30	45	8	15	30	45	9	15	30	45	...
ACTIVITY A01 Sleep																									
A02 Personal hygiene																									
A03 Food & Drink																									
A04 Transport																									
A05 Formal employment																									
A06 Household Production																									
A07 Study																									
A08 Housework																									
A09 Child care																									
A10 Elderly care																									
A11 Grocery purchase																									
A12 Medical service																									
A14 Voluntary activity																									
A15 Fitness																									
A16 Listen ratio/music																									
A17 Watch TV																									
A18 Reading																									
A19 Leisure & entertainment																									
A20 Socializing																									

Date of the Diary: / 05 / 2018 (Day of the Week)

INTERNET USAGE B01 Mobile phone/ pad					
B02 Other device					
B03 Did not use					
WITH WHOM C01 Alone & with Stranger					
C02 Age <60 household member					
C03 Age ≥60 household member					
C03 Friend/Relative					

Activity classification

1st Tier	2nd Tier	Descriptive
1		**SNA Productive Activities**
	11	Formal employment
	12	Household Production
2		**Non-SNA Productive Activities**
	21	Housework
	22	Childcare
	23	Elderly care
	24	Grocery purchase
	25	Voluntary activity
3		*Study*
	31	Study
4		*Free Time*
	41	Fitness
	42	Listen ratio/ music
	43	Watch TV
	44	Reading
	45	Leisure & entertainment
	46	Socializing
5		**Personal activities**
	51	Sleep
	52	Personal hygiene
	53	Food & Drink
	54	Medical service
6		**Transportation**
	61	Transport

References

Chiou, Y. S. (2009). A time use survey derived integrative human-physical household system energy performance model. *Paper presented at the 26th Conference on Passive and Low Energy Architecture*, Quebec City, Canada.

Dong, X., & An, X. (2015). Gender patterns and value of unpaid care work: Findings from China's first large-scale time use survey. *Review of Income and Wealth, 61*(3), 540–560. doi: 10.1111/roiw.12119.

Druckman, A., Buck, I., Hayward, B., & Jackson, T. (2012). Time, gender and carbon: A study of the carbon implications of British adults' use of time. *Ecological Economics*, *84*, 153–163. doi: 10.1016/j.ecolecon.2012.09.008.

Gravetter, F. J., & Wallnau, L. B. (2016). *Statistics for the behavioral science* (10th ed. Vol. 1). Cengage Learning.

National Bureau of Statistics. (2009). *Time-use patterns in China: Abstract of the 2008 time-use survey.* Retrieved from

National Bureau of Statistics. (2019). *Where has time gone? Statistical data of China's 2018 time-use survey.* Beijing: China Statistics Press.

National Bureau of Statistics. (2020). Data enquiry: Employment. Retrieved from http://data.stats.gov.cn/

National Bureau of Statistics of China. (2020). Data enquiry: transportation and post. Retrieved from https://data.stats.gov.cn/

Robinson, J. P., & Martin, S. (2011). Time use as a social indicator. In K. C. Land, C. M. Alex, & M. Joseph Sirgy (Eds), *Handbook of social indicators and quality of life research* (pp. 159–179). Dordrecht: Springer.

SEPA. (2006). *A letter on signing up liability contracts of major pollutants.* Beijing, China. http://www.sepa.gov.cn/info/gw/bgth/200702/t20070201_100504.htm

Tso, G. (2003). A study of domestic energy usage patterns in Hong Kong. *Energy*, *28*(15), 1671–1682. doi: 10.1016/s0360-5442(03)00153-1

Wang, Q., Ding, X., Lu, T., & Gu, N. (2012). *Digitality and materiality of new media: Online TV watching in China. Paper presented at the Proceedings of the SIGCHI Conference on Human Factors in Computing Systems*, Texas, USA.

Yao, C., Chen, C., & Li, M. (2012). Analysis of rural residential energy consumption and corresponding carbon emissions in China. *Energy Policy*, *41*, 445–450. doi: 10.1016/j.enpol.2011.11.005

Zheng, X., Wei, C., Qin, P., Guo, J., Yu, Y., Song, F., & Chen, Z. (2014). Characteristics of residential energy consumption in China: Findings from a household survey. *Energy Policy*, *75*, 126–135. doi: 10.1016/j.enpol.2014.07.016.

3 Estimating residential electricity and CO_2 intensity of time-use activity

3.1 Estimating energy intensity of time use

In our contemporary society, energy is a necessity that supports our day-to-day lives (Cleveland & Ayres, 2004). It powers our water, food, comfort, sanitation, recreation, and basic needs. It is embedded in almost all of our daily activities from wherever we are. In workplaces and schools, it operates equipment, lights up rooms, and provides us with thermal comfort. In transportation, it moves vehicles, trains and planes to take us to our destinations. At home, it heats up our meals, boils hot water for our baths and showers, and turns on the television for our entertainment. However, most of our current energy demand is met by fossil fuels, leading to CO_2 emission and environmental problems. To address this issue, a range of policies and studies on energy consumption have been introduced and conducted. However, they are mainly based on econometric and technical approaches. Energy efficiency standards, time-of-use tariffs, and other measures in line with these concepts have been primarily adopted and implemented (Newsham & Bowker, 2010; Office of Energy Efficiency & Renewable energy, 2020). Demand-side management has only begun to receive more attention as a complementary approach in the last two decades (Swan & Ugursal, 2009). Initiatives like social marketing and bill feedback have been introduced more often to change energy-related behavioral factors such as attitudes, norms, knowledge and skills (Fischer, 2008; Karlin, Zinger, & Ford, 2015; Meyer & Bäumer, 2020; Vandenbroele, Vermeir, Geuens, Slabbinck, & Van Kerckhove, 2020).

Time-use perspective energy consumption studies are also one of the emerging demand-side focused studies. However, they are often hampered by the lack of direct data on the energy or CO_2 intensity of activities, i.e., energy consumption or CO_2 emission per hour per person. Current time-perspective energy consumption studies generally

DOI: 10.4324/9780429291708-3

adopt two methods in estimating electricity and CO_2 intensity of activities. The first method uses energy use bill data, household expenditure survey data and environmentally extended input-output tables to estimate direct and indirect intensities of activities. The second one estimates direct intensities based on the power consumption characteristics of a list of commonly owned household appliances.

In the first method, time-use data are used to assess and quantify the impacts of individuals' everyday activities on material consumption. Studies often measured both direct intensity, i.e., the amount of resource consumed directly per hour of an activity, and indirect intensity, i.e., the amount of resourced consumed indirectly to produce the goods or services required by an hour of an activity (Jalas, 2009). One of the most commonly used measures of intensity estimation was proposed by Jalas (2002). In his study, he estimated Finnish direct intensity of activities from time-use survey data and energy bill data collected from the utilities, and the indirect intensities from time-use survey data, household expenditure survey data, and environmental extended input-output tables.

Using this method, Jalas (2002) first reconstructed the direct and indirect energy intensities of fourteen household activities for two-person Finnish households. In the following years, he and his colleagues extended the method to discuss the time-use rebound effects of time-saving technologies (Jalas, 2009), to explore the ecological impacts of urbanization (Heinonen, Jalas, Juntunen, Ala-Mantila, & Junnila, 2013a, 2013b; Wiedenhofer, Smetschka, Akenji, Jalas, & Haberl, 2018), and to explain the annual shift in energy consumption (Jalas, 2005; Jalas & Juntunen, 2015). Similar methods have been applied in studying energy consumption and CO_2 emissions of everyday life in other countries, such as Sweden (Isaksson & Ellegård, 2015), the United Kingdom (Druckman, Buck, Hayward, & Jackson, 2012), and the United States (Fitzgerald, Schor, & Jorgenson, 2018). However, as Jalas and Juntunen (2015) pointed out, there were two main limitations to the method. First, since time-use data and expenditure data were obtained from different datasets, the allocation of consumption expenditures to activities could only be based on guesses about good and services usage during activities. Some less straightforward, but frequently co-occurring usages, such as watching television while having meals (Lund & Gronow, 2014), may be omitted. Second, in the calculation of direct intensity, some high energy-consuming appliances such as refrigerators, space heaters, and air conditioners were excluded because of their unclear linkage to household activities, resulting in a large proportion of unexplained energy consumption.

To overcome these data limitations, Yu, Yang, Zhao, and Tan (2020) examined the casual relationship between time-use behaviors and residential energy consumption in China. In their study, they modified the existing time-use survey by adding a dimension of household equipment to collect simultaneously time-use and appliance data. The survey covered a small to medium sample of 466 households, and their findings identified the most energy-consuming activity (cooking), time-period (18:00–19:00), and demographic groups (rural elderly women) in China. However, although Yu et al. (2020)'s approach was able to offer more accurate data, it is difficult to replicate and scale up to a representative level with the constraints of research resources, and more importantly, it cannot provide insights into historical shifts of residential energy consumption and their evolved relationship with individuals' everyday life.

The second method focuses is on the timing of the daily electricity demand instead. They have higher requirements for temporal resolution of electricity intensities of activities, but lower requirements for their details and focus only on direct intensities. Time-use here no longer resembles the main body of research as in ecological economics but is an input factor representing the behavioral component of household electricity demand in their bottom-up electricity profile models. Its foundation was traced to a conference paper—Capsso, Gratteiri, Lamedica, and Prudenzi (1994). The paper presented the first hourly interval bottom-up activity-based model that incorporated inputs from both behavioral and engineering dimensions. Since then, further modifications and modeling approaches have been proposed; and of all these models, the high resolution energy demand model of Richardson, Thomson, Infield, and Clifford (2010) and the high-resolution stochastic model of domestic activity patterns and electricity demand of Widén and Wäckelgård (2010) were the two most frequently used models. They both constructed ten-minute resolution residential electricity load profiles using time-use data, but their methods for converting the data into the load curve were slightly different.

In Richardson et al. (2010)'s model, electricity demand per ten minutes was reconstructed using two variables obtained from time-use survey and the power consumption characteristics of a list of commonly owned household appliances. The two time-use variables— active occupancy, i.e., the number of occupants at home and active, and daily activity profile, i.e., the probability of occupants doing an activity at a given time of the day—were indicators of occupants' behaviors at home. They were employed to capture intra-day fluctuations and to model the demands along two key dimensions: one, general fluctuations induced by natural and social temporal rhythms, namely lower demand at night and higher demand during the day; and two, specific variations caused by the habitual behaviors of occupants, such as watching television at evening and showering in the morning. Widén and Wäckelgård (2010)'s model, on the other hand, viewed intra-day fluctuations not only as a result of occupant behaviors, but of their interaction with the temporal characteristics of power consumption of household appliances. In their estimation of electricity consumption, they divided the appliances into six groups based on their temporal characteristics and developed specific model routines for each group. This then allowed a better reflection of the fluctuations caused by household appliances, especially those like dishwashers and washing machines that have fluctuating consumption during the working cycle. Both the modeling results of Richardson et al. (2010)' and Widén and Wäckelgård (2010) were validated with small samples of measurement data and reported good correlations in main indicators.

Table 3.1 provides a brief summary of the characteristics of time-use perspective energy research in ecological the first and second

Table 3.1 Methods for estimating energy intensity of time use

	First Method	*Second Method*
Study focus	Direct and indirect ecological impact of individuals' everyday activities	High-resolution electricity demand, intra-day fluctuations
Data requirement	Time-use data Energy use bill data Household expenditure survey data Environmentally extended input-output tables	Time-use data Power characteristics of a list of commonly owned appliances
Strength	Allow the investigation of both direct and indirect intensities of activities Cover all kinds of material consumption, including energy, water, CO_2 emission, etc. Facilitate further explanatory analysis on over-year shifts in consumption	Estimate the electricity demand at very high temporal resolution Facilitate a better understanding of intra-day fluctuation in electricity demand Validate with real measurement with good correlations in key indicators
Weakness	Fail to take account of some high energy-consuming appliances	Cover only direct residential consumption

method for estimating electricity and CO_2 emissions. Given the different focus of the methods, their use of time-use data also differed. The first method used it to quantify the ecological impacts of individuals' everyday activities, while the second used it to capture intra-day fluctuations in electricity demand and to model high-resolution profiles. Each approach has its own strengths and weaknesses. Drawing from these two disciplines, this study develops a bottom-up approach for constructing electricity and CO_2 intensity of activities and is presented in the next section.

3.2 A bottom-up approach for constructing electricity and CO_2 intensity

We devise a bottom-up approach to construct direct residential electricity intensity of activities. CO_2 intensity is further calculated according to the CO_2 emission factor of electricity. Activities and electric appliances are first matched to understand how electricity is consumed for engaging time for an activity.

3.2.1 *Matching electric appliances with activities*

A common factor of residential energy consumption survey and time use data is first created using the concept of active occupancy introduced by Richardson et al. (2010) It reflects the presence and the activeness of occupants at home, which have been often considered to be the root causes of intra-day variations in residential electricity demand (Richardson, Thomson, & Infield, 2008; Torriti, 2017; Yao, Chen, & Li, 2012). It has been known in several versions, describing in varying degrees of details (McKenna, Krawczynski, & Thomson, 2015). This study adopts the most commonly used three-state model to cover all the necessary details of the presence and the activeness of occupants that may affect residential energy consumption. It describes the occupants' situations at home at a given time in terms of three occupancy statuses: (i) actively-occupied, i.e., the occupant is at home and active, (ii) passively-occupied, i.e., the occupant is at home, but sleeping, and (iii) absent, i.e., the occupant is not at home (Richardson et al., 2008; Richardson et al., 2010). Activities in the time-use survey and household appliances in the residential energy consumption survey were then reclassified to produce common factors for bridging the two datasets (Table 3.2).

Household appliances in the residential energy consumption survey are converted to occupancy status depending on their power

Table 3.2 Activity-appliance matching

Operation Mode of Appliance	Appliance (α)	Activity (j)	Detailed Activities
Background; 24 hours per day	Refrigerator Freezer	Absence from residence	All activities that take place away from residence
		All in-residence activities	All in-residence activities
Occupancy-related; All in-residence hours	Air conditioner (central; window; split) Oil filled electric radiator Electric heater Electric radiant floor heating Fan Light	Sleep	Sleep (passively occupied; all occupancy-related appliances are matched except light)
		All other in-residence activities	All other in-residence activities (actively occupied, including all below)

(Continued)

Table 3.2 (Continued)

Operation Mode of Appliance	Appliance (α)	Activity (j)	Detailed Activities
Activity-related; Related to in-residence activities	Instant water heater	Personal care	Showering/Bathing
	Television	Watching television	Watching television
	Computer (desktop, laptop, tablet)	Leisure and Socializing	Using computer technology for reading or audio; Computer games; Surfing the Internet; Work-related activities: Study-related activities
	Office equipment (All-in-one printer, printer, Fax machine, Copier, Scanner)	Paid Work Study	In-residence Paid Work In-residence Study
	Electric stove Cooker Microwave oven Oven Bread machine High pressure cooker	Unpaid work	Preparing and serving food
	Clothes washer Clothes dryer	Unpaid work	Washing clothes; Drying, ironing and storing clothes
	Storage water heater	Personal care	Showering/Bathing

consumption characteristics. An appliance is classified as 'Background appliance' if it automatically runs 24 hours a day, independent of the presence and activeness of the occupant. Otherwise, it is reclassified as 'Occupancy-related appliance' if it is only switched on when the occupant is at home, or as 'Activity-related appliance' if it is only switched on when the occupant does certain activity.

The reclassified activities and appliances are further matched according to their occupancy statuses identified in the previous step and the usage relationships found in previous empirical studies (Table 3.2). Appliances categorized as Activity-related are matched to actively occupied activities according to their function (Jalas, 2002, 2005, 2009). For example, televisions are assigned to watching television, storage and instantaneous water heaters are assigned to showering/bathing, and electric stoves are assigned to meal preparation. Yet, high-consumption appliances, which are not explicitly related to activities, are not excluded, as in the previous studies, but rather, as in Widén and Wäckelgård (2010), Background appliances such as refrigerators and freezers and occupancy-related appliances such as air conditioners and electric heaters are matched to all activities in absent, actively- and passively-occupied statuses. Some multifunctional appliances, such as computers and office equipment, are assigned to more than one activity. However, it is important to note that these matches are intended to cover typical use cases only. Specific use behaviors, such as leaving the TV on as white noise during work, are not discussed in this book.

Table 3.2 further differentiates various time-consuming activities between in-residence and absent from residence. All those not-in-residence activities are categorized into one activity j here, namely "Absent from residence". Others still follow the same categories as in Chapter 2 but refer to in-residence activities only.

3.2.2 *Electricity intensity*

Electricity intensity (Wh/hour/person) or CO_2 intensity (grams CO_2/hour/person) of activity refers to the amount of electricity consumption or CO_2 emission per hour for one person to be engaged in an activity. It is calculated as the product of electricity intensity of all appliances that have matched with the activity and CO_2 emission factor of electricity. As for the different electricity consumption characteristics of each groups of occupancy statuses, we develop specific formulas for each group when calculating their electricity consumptions and CO_2 emissions, as in Widén and Wäckelgård (2010).

$$CI_j^i = EI_j^i \cdot EF = \sum_\alpha \frac{N_\alpha^i \cdot P_\alpha^i \cdot T_\alpha^i \cdot M_{\alpha,j}}{U_j^i \cdot \sum_j \left(T_j^i \cdot M_{\alpha,j} \right)} \cdot EF \qquad (3.1)$$

Equation 3.1 Electricity/CO_2 intensity of activity.

i: Individuals of Chinese residents. Due to data constraints, this study can only differentiate the variables in this equation in a binary manner between urban and rural residents. In other words, they take average values in urban and rural China, respectively, across individuals and households;

j: Activity;

α: Electric appliance;

CI_j^i: CO_2 intensity of activity j in urban/rural China i (grams CO_2/hour/person, or g CO_2/h/person);

EI_j^i: Electricity intensity of activity j in urban/rural China i (Watt-h/h/person, or W/person);

EF: Emission factor of electricity (kg CO_2/kWh, or g CO_2/Wh). The values in 2008 and 2018 were 898 and 681 g CO_2/Wh, respectively (International Energy Agency, 2010, 2020);

N_α^i: Average ownership of appliance α per household in urban/rural China i;

P_α^i: Power rating of appliance α in urban/rural China i (W);

T_α^i: Hours per day for appliance α in operation in urban/rural China i (h/day);

$M_{\alpha,j}$: Matching between appliance α and activity j, or whether activity j uses appliance α. It is binary, 1 for being matched and 0 for not (Table 3.2);

U_j: Number of people who do activity j together in urban/rural China i. For activity "*Absence from residence*", this variable indicates the average size of a household;

T_j^i: Hours per day for activity j for individual i (h/day). Essentially T_j^i here refers to the average time-use patterns in urban/rural China as examined in Chapter 2. Even for those activity-related appliances, $T\alpha$ and T_j^i may not be the same. $\sum_j T_j^i = 24$.

3.3 Data

Our approach makes use of three major data sources for constructing electricity & CO_2 intensity of activities: the Chinese time-use survey, the Chinese residential energy consumption survey and the Baseline emission factors of China calculated from International Energy Agency (2010, 2020). In this section, we introduce the latter two sources and discuss how they adopted for our calculations (See Chapter 2 for the Chinese time-use survey).

3.3.1 The Chinese Residential Energy Consumption Survey (CRECS)

Residential Energy Consumption Surveys are usually stand-alone surveys that provide an account of energy consumption in the residential sector, enabling government and energy-related agencies to better identify energy problems, forecast future consumption, and design energy strategies (US Energy Information Administration, 1998). It was first conducted in 1979 as the Interim Nation Energy Consumption Survey in the United States; and in the late 1980s it was incorporated into the official survey and has been conducted by US Energy Information Administration every three years. It has also gained attention in other developed and developing countries. In 2008, in cooperation with all its members, Eurostat conducted a survey to collect residential energy data, such as energy consumption by end-use, expenditure on energy commodities, unit consumption, penetration of energy efficiency technologies (Eurostat, 2013). In the last decades, developing countries like Kosovo and Thailand have also carried out their surveys with the financial assistance from international organizations (Bowen, Myers, Myderrizi, Hasaj, & Halili, 2013).

Unlike time-use surveys, there have been no international standard or guideline for residential energy consumption surveys. They have, nevertheless, been implemented more or less in the same way in different countries and institutions (Zheng et al., 2014b). Most of them defined a residential unit as primary residence of the sampled household head to collect data in the category of energy, dwellings, and household characteristics. The detailed data items collected in each survey varied slightly, but generally included energy expenditure, appliance ownership and characteristics in the energy category, square footage, number of rooms, and insulation in the dwelling category, and number of household members, family status, and income levels in the household category. Lastly, data collection methods varied, ranging from computer-assisted telephone surveys to postal questionnaires and face-to-face interviews.

In China, the development of residential energy statistics is still at an introductory stage. The only government statistics available are the national and provincial residential energy consumption in the energy balance sheet. Individual-level data—essential to understanding residential energy consumption patterns—is rare. There has been only one residential energy consumption survey (CRECS) that was conducted by the Renmin University of China in 2012 and could provide a glimpse into the energy consumption situations in Chinese households. From December 2012 to March 2013, the survey collected data from 1,450 households in 27 selected provinces (Figure 3.1). A total of 120 undergraduate interviewers were recruited to sample and carry out the survey in their hometown based on the following four criteria: (i) The sampled households must be able to provide a 2012 electricity bill or record of electricity expenditure; (ii) The sampled households must consume energy primarily for domestic needs and cannot involve any form of production; (iii) The sampled households must have lived in their current residence for more than six months in 2012; (iv) Only one household can be sampled from the same community.

Figure 3.1 The 27 sampled provinces in the 2012 Chinese Residential Energy Consumption Survey.

(Zheng et al., 2014a, 2014b)

To ensure the data quality, each interviewer received a one-day training session on questionnaires, interview techniques, and equipment use. GPS devices and smartphones were used to record the exact location of the sampled household. Post-adjustment testing and validity testing were also performed (Zheng et al., 2014a).

Questionnaire: The questionnaire for the 2012 CRECS was designed with reference to the US Residential Energy Consumption Survey (Zheng et al., 2014a, 2014b). It comprises 324 questions in six areas: household demographics, dwelling characteristics, household appliances, space heating and cooling, use of private transportation, and electricity billing (Table 3.3); and is used as the basis for reconstructing the electricity intensity of an activity. All the electric appliances covered in the survey are reclassified into three occupancy groups and matched to relevant activities. The electricity intensity of each appliance is then calculated based on specific formula for its occupancy group, by its average type, size, year of purchase, energy label, power rate, usage frequency, and duration per use collected from the survey population. If a certain information of an appliance is missing, it will be estimated based on external data, such as China Energy Label standards and online market information (Table 3.4).

Profile of the samples: The descriptive statistics of respondents' demographics distribution and its comparison with the 2013 China Statistical Yearbook are given in Tables 3.4 and 3.5. The samples contain respondent of different provinces, residences (urban/rural), household sizes, income levels, and dwelling sizes; and the distributions have been slightly varied than the 2013 NBS. Most respondents (66%) lived from north, while only 34% were from the south. Its distribution across provinces was comparable to that of the NBS, with differences of less than 5% in all provinces except Guangdong and Shandong. Some greater differences between the two statistics were, meanwhile, found in their household characteristics. The sample population in CRECS were more likely to live in cities, have lower household sizes, higher income and larger dwellings. The share of urban residents in CRECS was 80.5%, which is 27.9% higher than that of the NBS. The average household size were 2.6 persons, 0.25 persons lower than the national average. Respondents were also more affluent than the national average, with urban and rural households earning more than RMB$39,500 and RMB$18,300 more annual than the national figures. In addition, the dwelling size of the urban sampled households was larger than average by 2.03m^2, while that of rural respondents was smaller by 8.95m^2. To minimize the errors caused by these differences, the dataset is weighted by household characteristics and population distribution in further analyses.

Table 3.3 List of variables in the 2012 Chinese Residential Energy
Consumption Survey (Zheng et al., 2014a, 2014b)

Areas	Variables
Household Demographics	• Household size • Demographics of household member: Relationship to householder, Gender, Age, Year of birth, Occupation, Nation, Education attainment, Number of months living at home in 2012
Dwelling Characteristics	• Urban/rural area • Building types • Number of rooms • Year started living • Construction year • Construction materials • Dwelling size
Household Appliances	• Type of appliance • Fuel in use • Year of purchase • Energy efficiency grade • Power rate (if applicable) • Frequency of usage • Duration per use
Space Heating and Cooling	• Type of space heating/ cooling in use • Fuel in use • Year of Purchase • Energy efficiency grade • Duration of use in 2012 • Duration per use • Cost burden
Use of Private Transportation	• Accessibility of home to nearby facilities • Transport behaviors of household member related to Public transport, Private car, Motorcycle
Electricity Billing, Metering, and Pricing Options	• Household annual income and expenditure • Basic information of electricity bill • Electricity expenditure in 2012 • Electricity price • Expenditure for other energy-related products

Table 3.4 Population distribution by province in the 2012 Chinese Residential Energy Consumption Survey and the 2012 annual national sample surveys of population (National Bureau of Statistics, 2013; Zheng et al., 2014a, 2014b)

Provinces	2012 CTUS	NBS 2013	Provinces	2012 CTUS	NBS 2013
% over 27 sampled provinces					
Anhui	2.9%	4.9%	Inner Mongolia	2.8%	2.0%
Beijing	5.0%	1.7%	Jiangxi	1.4%	3.7%
Chongqing	2.1%	2.4%	Jilin	5.2%	2.3%
Fujian	3.2%	3.1%	Liaoning	1.6%	3.6%
Gansu	1.4%	2.1%	Ningxia	1.4%	0.5%
Guangdong	0.4%	8.7%	Shandong	15.3%	7.9%
Guangxi	3.0%	3.8%	Shanghai	4.6%	1.9%
Guizhou	1.4%	2.9%	Shanxi	3.8%	3.0%
Hainan	0.1%	0.7%	Sichuan	2.6%	6.6%
Hebei	4.5%	6.0%	Tianjin	1.4%	1.2%
Heilongjiang	3.0%	3.1%	Xinjiang	1.8%	1.8%
Henan	9.2%	7.7%	Yunnan	2.0%	3.8%
Hubei	9.5%	4.7%	Zhejiang	2.3%	4.5%
Hunan	8.2%	5.4%			

Table 3.5 Profile of household characteristics in the 2012 Chinese Residential Energy Consumption Survey and the 2012 annual national sample surveys of population (National Bureau of Statistics, 2013; Zheng et al., 2014a, 2014b)

Variables	2012 CRECS			NBS 2013		
	Total	Urban	Rural	Total	Urban	Rural
Urban Ratio	80.5%	—	—	52.6%	—	—
Household Size	2.6	2.57	2.95	3.02	2.86	3.88
Annual Household Income (RMB$10,000)	9.78	10.98	4.90		7.03	3.07
Dwelling Size (m²)	103.73	96.15	134.98		94.12	143.93

3.3.2 *Mending the mismatched datasets*

This study uses the CTUS and the CRECS as the input data to reconstruct an activity-based residential energy consumption profile of Chinese. However, the two datasets were collected in different years (2008 and 2018 for CTUS; 2012 for CRECS), so to eliminate data bias, we examined the changes in time-use patterns, appliance characteristics, and household demographic characteristics—the three key input elements of our reconstructing approach—between 2008, 2012 and 2018. From data in the Chinese Family Panel Studies, the China National Statistical Yearbooks, and the China Energy Label Standards, we found that the major changes between 2008, 2012 and 2018 were primarily in appliance and household characteristics, but not much in time-use patterns. For this, we will process and weight the data based on the expected changes in appliance and household characteristics to estimate the appliance consumption in 2008 and 2018 and to combine with CTUS for modeling the activity-based residential electricity consumption profiles for the two years. In addition, we understand that there might be a slight possibility that differences in appliances use may influence residents' time-use patterns, vice versa, but as this is not the focus of this book, so it will not be considered in the subsequent data processing.

Differences in time-use patterns: Given that the CTUS is conducted every ten years and data are currently only available for 2008 and 2018, it is difficult to compare the actual changes in time-use patterns of Chinese residents in 2008 and 2018 with those in 2012. Fortunately, there is another survey—the Chinese Family Panel Studies—that has collected some basic information on the time-use of Chinese residents every two years, allowing us to get a glimpse of the changes between the three years studied. The survey is a longitudinal survey conducted by the Institute of Social Science Survey at Peking University. Every two years the same group of respondents is interviewed to to investigate the changes in well-being of the Chinese population, including general activity time (ISSS of Peking University, 2018)

Based on their data, the time-use pattern of urban respondents was nearly identical between 2008 and 2018 (Figure 3.2). They were only small time shifts from watching TV to other leisure activities. Most of the variations was within 10%. The largest difference were only 9% in watching TV in the weekends, which accounted for only 2/7 in calculating time spent on watching TV on a typical day. Therefore, we assume that the temporal mismatch of the datasets does not cause any critical bias in terms of time use.

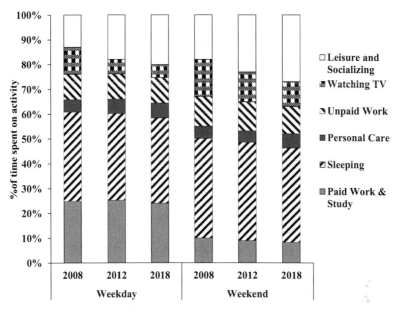

Figure 3.2 Changes in Chinese time-use pattern between 2008, 2012, and 2018. (ISSS of Peking University, 2018).

Difference in appliance characteristics: Appliance ownership, power rate, and daily usage are the three main appliance variables used in our reconstructing method. Below will review the changes in the first two appliance characteristics between 2008, 2012, and 2018. However, as for daily usage of appliance, since there were no relevant data collected, it is not possible to assess the changes between 2008, 2012, and 2018; therefore, we can only speculate that the daily usage of appliances was also relatively stable between these three years as in the time-use pattern.

Ownership of major appliances like refrigerators, air conditioners, washing machines, televisions, and computer has increased rapidly between the three years as recorded in the National Bureau of Statistics, 2009a, 2013, and 2019a (Figure 3.3). The largest change was in rural households, who owned more high electricity-consuming appliances such as air conditioners (increased by 158% from 2008 to 2012; 157% from 2012 to 2018) and refrigerators (increased by 123% from 2008 to 2012; 42% from 2012 to 2018). Their number of computers, washing machines, and televisions, and washing machines owned also increased significantly by 402%, 80%, and 18%, respectively. In contrast, the number of appliances owned by urban households remained relatively stable, with only air conditioners and computers gaining a bigger

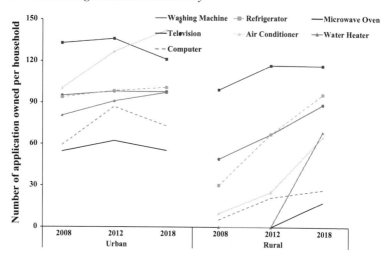

Figure 3.3 Changes of the number of seven major appliances owned per household between 2008, 2012, and 2018.

(National Bureau of Statistics, 2009a, 2013, 2019a).

increase of 10% and 7%, respectively. This echoes arguments in the empirical studies about the saturation of home appliances in Chinese urban households (Meier, Lin, Liu, & Li, 2004; Zhao, Li, & Ma, 2012).

Regarding appliance power rates, although there are no publicly available time-series data showing the change in power rates of appliances owned by Chinese households, we can get a general idea of the changes over the three years from the changes in Energy Label Standards. It is energy conservation program that records, publishes and regulates the energy efficiency level of household appliances in Chinese. It is a mandatory national standard that requires products of a range of household appliances, whether domestically produced and imported from abroad, to be tested to determine the energy efficiency level of the products, and recorded in a catalogue for public reference (China National Institution of Standardization, 2021). Based on the power consumption data from the catalogue, we found that there was an overall trend towards greater energy efficiency between 2008 and 2018, meaning that the appliance power rates needed to be reduced significant to main the same level of energy efficiency. For the two high electricity-consuming appliances, refrigerators and freezers, the required power rates to remain the same level decreased by 6.89% and 8.85% in 2012 and 28.42% and 17.94 in 2018, respectively (Figure 3.4).

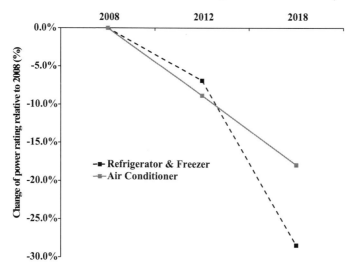

Figure 3.4 Changes of the power rate requirements of refrigerators, freezers and air conditioners in Chinese Energy Label Standards between 2008, 2012, and 2018.

(China National Institution of Standardization, 2021).

Difference in Household demographic characteristics: Household demographic characteristics are not direct input elements in our reconstructing approach, but as empirical studies have shown, they have a strong influence on one's time-use pattern and the characteristics of owned appliance. Therefore, we also examine changes in three key household characteristics—household size, income level, and dwelling size—to investigate their possible impacts to our consumption estimations.

As recorded in the National Statistics Yearbook, there have been substantial changes in household characteristics between 2008, 2012, and 2018 (Figure 3.5). The average household size decreased; smaller family has emerged to be the new dominant household type. The number of members per urban and rural household decreased to 0.05 and 0.13, respectively between 2008 and 2012; and between 2012 and 2018, it further decreased to 2.85 persons and 3.70 persons per urban and rural households. Moreover, Chinese households have become increasingly affluent over the years. Their annual household income of urban and rural households increased by 56% and 66% from 2008 to 2012, and 60% and 85% from 2012 to 2018. In particular, urban households experienced a rise that was twice as high as rural households.

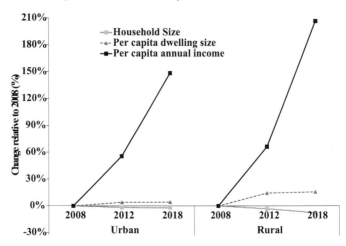

Figure 3.5 Changes in household size, per-capita dwelling size and annual income in urban and rural households between 2008, 2012, and 2018.

(National Bureau of Statistics, 2009a, 2013, 2019a).

Lastly, per-capita dwelling size have also increased by 4% and 16% from 2008 to 2018 in urban and rural households, respectively. This trend of increasingly affluent but smaller Chinese households has been likely to lead to an increase in per-capita appliance ownership as well as in electricity consumption.

3.4 Changes in electricity and CO_2 intensity of daily activities between 2008 and 2018

This section presents all the weighted input factors used to reconstruct the activity-based residential electricity and CO_2 intensity. Estimates for each of the two components—appliance characteristics, and sharing characteristics—are reported by (i) year, (ii) urban and rural residence, and (iii) activity category.

3.4.1 Appliance characteristics in 2008 and 2018

Appliance ownership, power rate, and daily usage are the three appliance variables used in our reconstruction approach. Their values for 2008 and 2018 listed below are estimated by weighted data from 2012 CRECS (China National Institution of Standardization, 2021; National Bureau of Statistics, 2009a, 2013, 2019a).

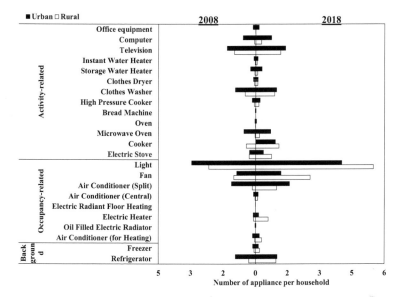

Figure 3.6 Average number of electric appliances in urban and rural households, by 2008 and 2018.

Appliance ownership: The ownership of the 29 common household electric appliances in Chinese households has grown from 2008 to 2018 (Figure 3.6). Those new technology appliances, such as computers and office equipment, saw the largest increases. This was followed by thermal comfort-related appliances, while traditional appliances like refrigerators, televisions, and washing machines had the smallest increases. Urban-rural differences also narrowed considerably. In 2018, both types of households owned almost the same number of refrigerators, freezers, televisions, and cookers. Only in computers, office equipment, and air conditioners did urban households still own significantly more than rural households. Meanwhile, it is interesting to note that rural households owned markedly higher number in lights, fans, and electric heaters.

Appliance power rate: Appliance power rate is estimated based on the average appliance characteristics of size, type, year of purchase, brand, and the energy efficiency label obtained from CRECS, in calibration for changes in power rate requirements listed in the 2008, 2012, and 2018 energy labelling standards.

Between 2008 and 2018, the power rates of most appliances fell by less than 450W. There were only two high electricity-consuming appliances—instant water heaters and air conditioners—that have shown

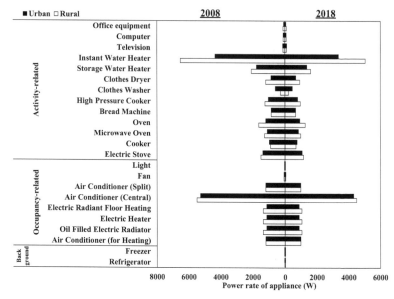

Figure 3.7 Average power rate of appliances in urban and rural households, by 2008 and 2018.

relatively large improvements in energy efficiency, at around 900 W to 1,500 W. The differences between urban and rural households were also not significant, at below than 300 W in 2008 and 250 W in 2018 for most appliances. They were only slightly more pronounced urban-rural difference in the instant water heaters (2,176W in 2008; 1,686 in 2018), ovens (436 W in 2008; 338 W in 2018), clothes washers (315W in 2008; 244 W in 2018), and clothes dryers (326 W in 2018 and 253 W in 2018).

Appliance daily usage: Daily usage of the 29 appliances, the average number of hours of the appliance being in operation within a day, was estimated based on data obtained from the 2012 Chinese Residential Energy Consumption Survey, and was assumed to have no difference between 2008 and 2018.

Regarding the eight occupancy-related appliances, the most frequently used appliance was the lights, with an average of about five hours per day (Figure 3.8). Other HVAC appliances were while used for much less hours at only 0.5 to 1 hour per day. Between urban and rural households, their average usages were similar.

For activity-related appliances, the most commonly used appliances were televisions (~2 hour/day), storage water heaters (~1 hour/day),

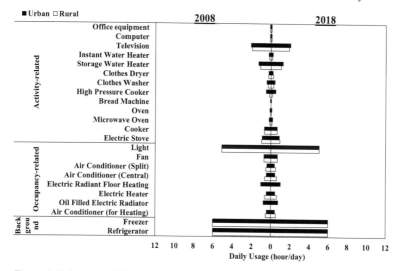

Figure 3.8 Average daily usage of appliances in urban and rural households, by 2008 and 2018.

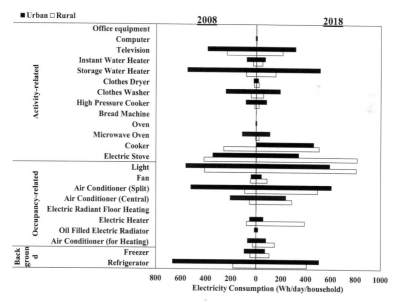

Figure 3.9 Average daily electricity consumption by appliance in urban and rural households, by 2008 and 2018.

electric shoves (~0.8 hour/day), and cookers (~0.6 hour/day) (Figure 3.8). Other nine appliances were used for less than 0.3 hour per day. The difference between urban and rural were also not significant, with the larger variations of urban households having a more often use of clothes washers (0.13 hours/day), storage electric water heaters (0.18 hours/day), microwave ovens (0.06 hours/day), and high-pressure cookers (0.35 hours/day), and less in electric stoves (0.06 hours/day), cookers (0.01 hours/day), and clothes dryers (0.05 hours/day)

Finally, background appliances such as refrigerators were assumed to operate 24/7, so their usage in hours per day for both urban and rural households was 24 hours/day.

Electricity consumption: The average daily household electricity consumption for each 27 appliances were estimated with above data of ownerships, power ratings, and daily usages of appliances in urban and rural households in 2008 and 2018.

From 2008 and 2018, that of urban and rural household showed a markedly different trend. Urban households' consumptions have decreased from an average of 4,497 Wh/household/day to 4,312 Wh/household/day, with a decrease of 4.1%. Rural household, while, consumed significantly more electricity from 2,014 Wh/household/day to 4,586 Wh/household/day, surpassing that of urban households during the decade.

By appliance, both urban and rural found to have the highest in consumption in 2018 in refrigerators (505 Wh/household/day for urban households; 407 Wh/household/day for rural households), spilt air conditioners (604 Wh/household/day for urban households; 493 Wh/household/day for rural households), lights (590 Wh/household/day for urban households; 805 Wh/household/day for rural households), and cookers (461 Wh/household/day for urban households; 506 Wh/household/day for rural households).

Combining the discussions in previous three sections, we may reveal the reasons of the differences. For the small changes in urban households' consumption, there might have two possible explanations: one is due to an offset between the growth in appliance ownership and the improvement in energy efficiency; and another is that urban appliances have been already saturated and most of the major appliances have lifetimes of ten years or more, which therefore have not benefited significantly from improvements in appliance efficiency and received only a reduction of 4.1%. However, for rural families, the situation was just the opposite. With the rapid development of China's rural economy over the decade, rural household could gradually afford purchasing more appliances and live a moderner life akin to that of urban dwellers. As a result, the average number of appliances they owned has increased dramatically, far outpacing the improvement in the average power rating of appliances, resulting an overall consumption even higher than those of urban households.

3.4.2 Sharing characteristics in 2008 and 2018

Another important step in our reconstruction approach is to convert household daily electricity consumption (Watt/day/household) to electricity intensity of activity at the individual level (Watt/day/person-hour). However, as mentioned earlier, activity-level data on appliance usage, including those required for the above conversion—the total number of household members involved in and the total time spent for the activities that involved the use of appliances—do not exist. Therefore, in order to perform the above conversion, some assumptions are made to categorize appliances into three operation modes—background (used 24/7), occupied-related (used only when the resident is at home) and activity-related (used only during specific activity), match the activity and appliance and estimate the data items in sharing characteristics at individual and activity level of each appliance based on their usage characteristics.

Number of household members involved in activities matched to an appliance: The number of household members involved in activities matched to each respective appliance is the main figure in converting daily household consumption into a per-capita value.

The estimation of the value for each appliance is based on their occupancy group. First, the background appliances which operate as their 24/7 and their electricity consumption is not affected by what the residents are being and doing, their electricity consumption is assumed to be shared equally by all members of the household. That is, the average household size in urban (2.92 in 2008; 2.46 in 2018) and rural household (4.03 in 2008; 2.36 in 2018) published in the China Statistics Yearbooks.

As for the occupancy-related and activity-related appliances, the number of member sharing the appliance are the average number of household members in the same room during all the passively- and actively-occupied, and specific matched activities estimated based on the data item of companion persons acquired from the time-use survey diary, respectively. However, it is important to note that because data on the companion person were not collected in the 2018 CTUS, the values for that year can only be estimated based on the 2008 CTUS values with adjustments based on the 2018 household size data.

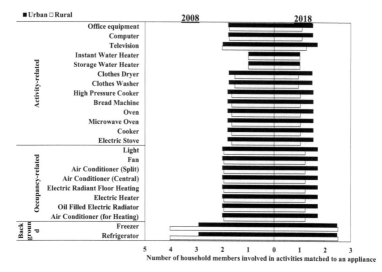

Figure 3.10 Average number of household members involving in activities matched to an appliance, by urban and rural residents, by 2008 and 2018.

The resulting estimates showed that in 2008, an average of 2.01 and 1.96 people in urban and rural household shared an occupancy-related applianced, while in 2018, that was 1.69 people and 1.66 people for urban and rural household, respectively. For activity-related appliance, the number of members sharing the appliance ranged from 1 to 2 and 1 to 2.02 in 2008 for urban and rural households, respectively, and from 1 to 1.52 and from 1 to 1.40 in 2018.

Overall, we can see that that appliances in 2018 were generally shared by fewer residents (Figure 3.10).

Time spent on the activities matched to an appliance: Time spent in the activities matched to an appliance, the sum of the average time spent on all the activities that matched that particular appliance, is another important element to convert daily household electricity consumption to electricity intensities of activities.

Its value for each appliance was again estimated according to the operation mode of the appliances. For background appliances, since they operated round-the-clock, it was matched to all activities and assigned with a value of 24 hours. Occupancy-related appliances were matched with all passively-, actively-occupied activities, and activity-related appliances were mated specific related activities. Unfortunately, the 2018 CTUS survey did not collected activity location. Their values can only be estimated based on the average time spent on their

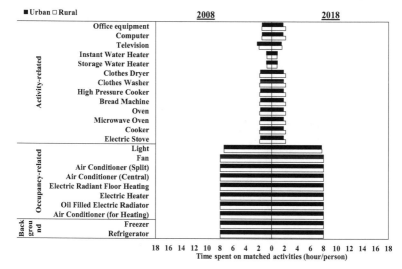

Figure 3.11 Average time spent on activities matched to an appliance, by urban and rural residents, by 2008 and 2018.

matched activities and calibrated with the indoor-outdoor activity ratio obtained from 2008 CTUS. In the post-calibrated results (Figure 3.11) it can be seen that the differences were only in activity-related appliances.

3.4.3 Reconstructed intensity of activity in 2008 and 2018

With the above listed three data on appliance characteristics and two on sharing characteristics, the electricity and CO_2 intensities of activities can be reconstructed. In addition, to obtain more accurate results, we added one extra procedure—calibrating with national statistics. This was to reduce the error caused by the lack of data. In the procedure, (i) the average daily residential electricity consumption is first obtained by multiplying the activity intensities estimated based the above five inputting data items with the average time spent on corresponding activities and (ii) the resulting electricity consumption is calibrated with the actual consumption from the Chinese Statistical Yearbook and Energy Statistic Yearbook (National Bureau of Statistics, 2009a, 2009b, 2019a, 2019b). The calibrated electricity intensity will be further used to multiply with the CO_2 emission factors to reconstruct the CO_2 intensity of activity, and in the next chapter to estimate the average residential daily electricity consumption and associated CO_2 emissions.

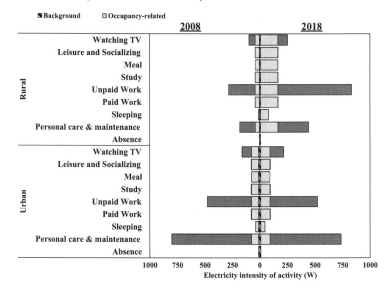

Figure 3.12 Electricity intensity of activity before calibration, by urban and rural residents, by 2008 and 2018.

Reconstructed electricity intensity of activity before calibration: The resulting electricity intensities of the nine activities exhibited considerable differences between urban and rural and between 2008 and 2018, especially for activity-related intensities. The biggest variations in activity-related intensities were in personal care and maintenance and unpaid work, which used high electricity-consuming appliances like instant electric water heater, oven, and cookers. In 2008, the urban-rural differences in activity-related electricity intensities of these two activities were 584 W and 157 W, respectively. In 2018, the difference between urban and rural have shrunken to 365 W in personal care and maintenance; and 235W for unpaid work.

A similar trend was also observed in occupancy-related intensities. The average occupancy-related intensities of urban and rural residents have increased from 2008 to 2018, with a much higher rate for rural residents, at 119 W. In 2018, Their average occupancy-related intensities has exceed that of urban residents by 74W. reaching 157W. has even exceeded that of urban residents by 74 W, reaching 157 W.

Overall, the ranks of activities based on the electricity intensities for urban and rural residents were the same in both 2008 and 2018. Urban residents demand the higher energy to do an hour of personal care and maintenance, unpaid work and watching television, while for rural residents, they were unpaid work, personal care and maintenance, and watching television. Leisure and socializing, meal, study, and paid work, which do not match with specific activity-related appliances, were the medium-intensive, and sleeping was the electricity-least intensive.

Calibration by per-capita daily residential consumption: To obtain more accurate results and eliminate errors from the data estimation, the above electricity intensity is calibrated with the actual per-capita residential daily consumption derived from the Chinese national statistics (National Bureau of Statistics, 2009a, 2009b, 2019a, 2019b). The estimated electricity intensity of each activities will first multiply with the corresponding average time spent, and sum it to obtain the average total per-capita daily electricity consumption. The actual per-capita residential daily consumption is calculated by dividing the year-end population by place of residence from the Chinese Statistical Yearbook with the final residential electricity consumption for urban and rural households from the Energy Statistical Yearbook.

Our estimates were generally aligned with the national statistics and had similar distributions by years and place of residence (Figure 3.13). They both showed that in 2008, urban residents had a higher per-capita daily electricity consumption than rural residents, but That is, in 2018, rural residents instead had generally higher consumption than urban residents. However, our preliminary estimates were higher than the national statistics. In 2008, our estimates were 122% and 52% higher than the national statistics for urban and rural residents, and in 2018, the differences were 52% and 72%. There were two possible explanations for our higher estimates. One was because of the quality of our data sources did not yet perfectly reflect the actual situation in China. For instance, the 2018 CRECS had limitations such as incomplete spatial coverage and small sample size. Or it indicated excessive matching of appliances to activities in our approach.

To ensure our estimates better reflected the actual situation, our estimated residential electricity intensities of all activities are proportionally scaled lower to match the value of national statistics. The post-calibrated electricity intensities of activities are shown in Figure 3.14 by year and place of residence.

Reconstructed CO_2 intensity of activity: The final step of our reconstructed approach is to estimate the CO_2 intensity of activities, by multiplying the calibrated electricity intensity of each activity with the Chinese emissions factor in 2008 and 2018 derived from International Energy Agency (2010, 2020). This factor represents the amount of

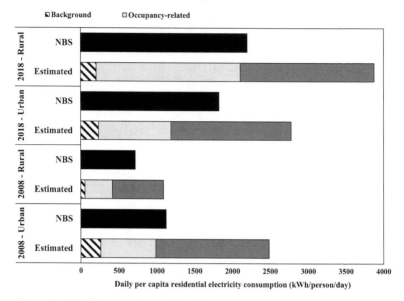

Figure 3.13 Daily per-capita residential electricity consumption derived from our estimation and from national statistics, by urban and rural residents, by 2008 and 2018.

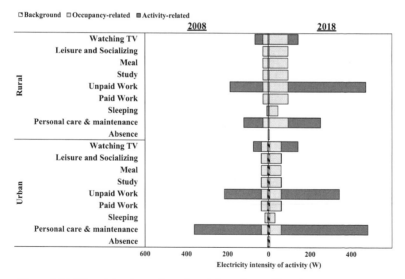

Figure 3.14 Electricity intensity of activity after calibration, by urban and rural residents, by 2008 and 2018.

CO_2 emissions from the consumption of one degree of electricity and are calculated by dividing the total emissions of the entire grid by the total electricity consumption.

The distribution of the resulting CO_2 intensities of activities highly resembled the electricity intensities of the activities. The biggest differences by years and residences were also found in between 2008 and 2018 the activity-related intensities in personal care and maintenance and unpaid work. The rise between 2008 and 2018 in activity-related and occupancy-related intensities of rural residents were also much more considerable than urban residents.

Changes in CO_2 intensities of activities were, however, smaller in extent than in electricity intensities. This might reflect the Chinese government's active efforts in CO_2 mitigation over the decade. In 2018, an hour of high-intensive activities—personal care and maintenance, unpaid work, and watching TV—in average emitted 328 gCO_2, 233 gCO_2, and 96 gCO_2 for urban residents, and 171 gCO_2, 321 gCO_2, 98 gCO_2 for rural residents. An hour of medium-intensive activities— leisure and socializing, meal, study, and paid work—emitted around 40 gCO_2 and 60 gCO_2 for urban and rural residents, respectively, while an hour of low-intensive activity of sleeping would be leaded to 21 gCO_2 for urban residents and 31 gCO_2 for rural residents (Figure 3.15 and Table 3.6).

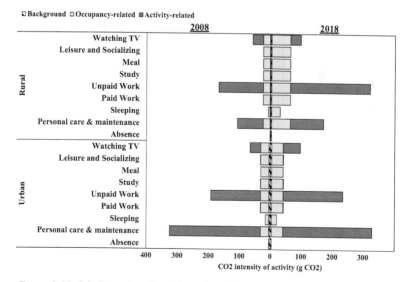

Figure 3.15 CO_2 intensity of activity after calibration, by urban and rural residents, by 2008 and 2018.

Table 3.6 Appliance variables collected in the 2012 Chinese Residential Energy Consumption Survey (National Bureau of Statistics, 2013; Zheng et al., 2014a, 2014b)

Household Appliance	Variables								External Data
	Number	Type	Size	Year of Purchase	Energy label	Power Rate	Usage Frequency per Use	Duration	
Background-related									
Refrigerator	✓	✓	✓	✓	✓				Energy Label Standard[1] (GB12021.2-1999; GB12021.2-2003; GB12021.2-2008)
Freezer	✓	✓	✓	✓	✓				
Occupancy-related									
Air Conditioner (Heating)	✓	✓					✓	✓	Energy Label Standard[1] (GB 12021.3-2004, GB 12021.3-2010)
Oil Filled Electric Radiator	✓	✓					✓	✓	Zheng et al. (2014a, 2014b) & Online Market Information[2]
Electric Heater	✓	✓					✓	✓	Zheng et al. (2014a, 2014b) & Online Market Information[2]
Electric Radiant Floor Heating	✓	✓					✓	✓	Zheng et al. (2014a, 2014b) & Online Market Information[2]
Air Conditioner (Central)	✓	✓	✓				✓	✓	Online Market Information[2]

Appliance							Data Source
Air Conditioner (Split)	✓	✓			✓	✓	Energy Label Standard[1] (GB 12021.3-2004, GB 12021.3-2010)
Fan	✓	✓			✓	✓	Energy Label Standard[1] (GB 12021.9-1989)
Light	✓				✓		Online Market Information[2]
Activity-related							
Time-saving							
Electric Stove	✓	✓		✓	✓	✓	
Cooker	✓	✓		✓	✓	✓	
Microwave Oven	✓	✓		✓	✓	✓	
Oven	✓	✓		✓	✓	✓	
Bread Machine	✓	✓		✓	✓	✓	
High Pressure Cooker	✓	✓		✓	✓	✓	
Clothes Washer	✓	✓	✓		✓	✓	Energy Label Standard[1] (GB 12021.4.1989; GB 12021.4.2004)
Clothes Dryer	✓	✓	✓		✓	✓	Online Market Information[2]
Storage Water Heater	✓	✓	✓		✓	✓	Energy Label Standard[1] (GB 21519-2008)

(Continued)

Table 3.6 (Continued)

Household Appliance	Variables								
	Number	Type	Size	Year of Purchase	Energy label	Power Rate	Usage Frequency	Duration per Use	External Data
Non Time-saving									
Instant Water Heater	✓			✓			✓	✓	Online Market Information[2]
Television	✓	✓	✓	✓	✓		✓		Energy Label Standard[1] (GB 12021.7-2005)
Computer (Desktop)	✓			✓	✓		✓		Zheng et al. (2014a, 2014b) & Online Market Information[2]
Computer (Laptop)	✓								Zheng et al. (2014a, 2014b) & Online Market Information[2]
Computer (Tablet)	✓								Zheng et al. (2014a, 2014b) & Online Market Information[2]
All-in-One Printer	✓								Energy Label Standard[1] (GB21521-2008)
Printer									Energy Label Standard[1] (GB21521-2008)
Fax Machine	✓								Online Market Information[2]
Copier	✓								Energy Label Standard[1] (GB21521-2008)

1 Estimated based on its ownership, characteristics (energy label, size, type and type of purchases) obtained from CRECS and energy coefficient from the energy labels standards.
2 Online market information refers to technical specification published by appliance producers.

Appendix I Comparison of activity categorization in this book, 2008 and 2018 Chinese time-use survey

This Book	2008 CTUS	2018 CTUS
Activity location: Not at home		
0　Absence	All activities (11–899)	All activities (11–899); Travel (A04)
Activity location: At home		
1　Personal care, maintenance	Personal hygienic activities (31), Showering/ Bathing (32), Grooming (33), Other personal hygienic activities (34), Smoking (50), Other personal care activities (60)	Personal hygiene (A02), Other personal activities (A13)
2　Sleeping	Night sleep/essential sleep (11), Incidental sleep/naps (12), Sleep in sick (13)	Sleep (A01)
3　Paid Work	Work, main work (111), Work, part work (112), Apprenticeship or Internship (113), Short breaks and interruption form work (114), Training and studies in related to work (115), Looking for work (116), Looking for/setting-up business (117), Other work-related activities (120), Growing of crops (210), Growing of trees (220), Farming of animals (230), Fishing and aquatic farming (240), Other household primary productive activities (250), Travel related to household primary productive activities (299), Processing of agricultural products (310), Processing of food products (320), Making beverages (330), Making textile, leather, and associated products (340), Crafting-making using non-metal materials (350), Other household secondary productive activities (360), Household construction activities (370), Other household construction activities (380), Travel related to household construction activities (399), Food vending and trading (410), Providing repair, installation, and maintenance services (420), Providing professional services (430), Providing personal care services (440), Transporting goods and passengers (450), Paid domestic services (460), Other household tertiary productive activities (470)	Employment (A05), Household Production (A06)

Continued

This Book	2008 CTUS	2018 CTUS
4 Unpaid Work	Preparing and serving food (511), Cleaning up after meal (512), Indoor cleaning (521), Outdoor cleaning (522), Washing clothes (531), Drying, ironing, and storing clothes (532), Mending and care of clothes (533), Care of grade (553), Daily pet care (551), Taking pets for veterinary care (552), Household decoration, maintenance, and repairing (561), Installation, servicing, and repair of household goods (562), Vehicle maintenance and minor repairs (563), Household management (570), Other domestic work-related activities (580)	Housework (A08), Grocery Purchase (A12), Physical care for child (A09), Education for child (A10), Physical care for adult member (A11), Voluntary work (A14)
5 Study	Attending classes and lectures (711), Breaks/waiting at place of general education (712), Self-study for distance education course work (713), Homework, course review, research, and activities (721), Additional study, non-formal education (730), Career/professional development training and studies (740), Other study-related activities (750)	Study (A07)
6 Meal	Eating a meal (21), Drinking other than with meal or snack (22), Eating snack (23)	Meal (A03)

This Book	2008 CTUS	2018 CTUS
7 Leisure and Socializing	Listening to radio (816), Listening to other audio media (817), Reading books (811), Reading periods (812), Reading other specific materials (813), Walking and running (821), Martial art (822), Aerobics, yoga, weight-training, and other fitness programmes (823), Ball games (824), Water sports (825), Other sports (826), Card games, board games (831), Religious activities (40), Using computer technology for reading or audio (818), Surfing the Internet (819), Computer games (832), Social/group games (833), Purchasing for collection (834), Performing arts (835), Attendance at movies (841), Core activities: time spent attending cultural, entertainment, and sports events Attendance at organized/mass cultural events (842), Attendance at shows (843), Attendance at sports events (844), Other leisure activities (860), Talking, conversing (851), Reading and writing mail (852), Other socializing activities (853)	Listening to radio/ music (A16), Reading book, magazine, etc (A18), Sport and fitness (A16), Other leisure activities (A19), Socializing (A20)
8 Watching TV	Watching television (814), Watching/listening to video programmes (815)	Watching TV (A17)

Appendix II Detailed description of appliance operation mode

Appliance Group (a)	Household Electric Appliance (m)	Justification
Background (0)	• Refrigerator • Freezer	*Technical feature:* Appliance in this group operates on its own technical cycle in 24/7; hence, I assumed their usage is unrelated to either the occupant's presence or the type of primary activity.
Occupancy-related (1)	• Air Conditioner • Oil Filled Electric Radiator • Electric Heater • Electric Radiant Floor Heating • Air Conditioner (Central) • Air Conditioner (Window) • Air Conditioner (Split) • Fan • Light	*Expected usage behavior:* As appliances in this group are mostly HVAC appliances that provide comfort to the occupant, rather than being devoted to specific activities like cooking, it is assumed that their usage depends on the occupant's presence, whilst not being a primary activity.
Activity-related (2)	• Electric Stove • Cooker • Microwave Oven • Oven • Bread Machine • High Pressure Cooker • Clothes Washer • Clothes Dryer • Storage Water Heater • Instant Water Heater • Television • Computer (Desktop) • Computer (Laptop) • Computer (Tablet) • Printer with Scanner • Printer; Fax Machine • Copier	*Expected usage behavior:* Appliances in this group serve for specific activity, like cooking and laundry; hence, it is assumed that their use depends on the type of active in-house activities undertaken.

References

Bowen, B. H., Myers, J. A., Myderrizi, A., Hasaj, B., & Halili, B. (2013). *Kosovo Household Energy Consumption*. Retrieved from

Capsso, A., Gratteiri, W., Lamedica, R., & Prudenzi, A.(1994). A bottom-up approach to residential load modeling. *IEEE Transactions on Power Systems*, *9*(2). doi: 10.1109/59.317650

China National Institution of Standardization. (2021). Record for China Energy Labels (备案公告查询). Retrieved from https://www.energylabelrecord.com

Cleveland, C. J., & Ayres, R. U. (2004). Preface. In C. J. Cleveland (Ed), *Encyclopedia of energy* (Vol. 1). Amsterdam; Boston: Elsevier Science

Druckman, A., Buck, I., Hayward, B., & Jackson, T. (2012). Time, gender and carbon: A study of the carbon implications of British adults' use of time. *Ecological Economics*, *84*, 153–163. doi: 10.1016/j.ecolecon.2012.09.008

Eurostat. (2013). *Manuals and Guidelines Manual for Statistics on Energy Consumption in Households*. Retrieved from

Fischer, C. (2008). Feedback on household electricity consumption: A tool for saving energy? *Energy Efficiency*, *1*(1), 79–104. doi: 10.1007/s12053-008-9009-7

Fitzgerald, J. B., Schor, J. B., & Jorgenson, A. K. (2018). Working hours and carbon dioxide emissions in the United States, 2007–2013. *Social Forces*, *96*(4), 1851–1874. doi: 10.1093/sf/soy014

Heinonen, J., Jalas, M., Juntunen, J. K., Ala-Mantila, S., & Junnila, S. (2013a). Situated lifestyles: I. How lifestyles change along with the level of urbanization and what the greenhouse gas implications are—A study of Finland. *Environmental Research Letters*, *8*(2), 025003. doi:10.1088/1748-9326/8/2/025003

Heinonen, J., Jalas, M., Juntunen, J. K., Ala-Mantila, S., & Junnila, S. (2013b). Situated lifestyles: II. The impacts of urban density, housing type and motorization on the greenhouse gas emissions of the middle-income consumers in Finland. *Environmental Research Letters*, *8*(3), 035050. doi:10.1088/1748-9326/8/3/035050

International Energy Agency. (2010). World Energy Outlook 2010. IEA, Paris, France.

International Energy Agency. (2020). World Energy Outlook 2020. IEA, Paris, France.

Isaksson, C., & Ellegård, K. (2015). Dividing or sharing? A time-geographical examination of eating, labour, and energy consumption in Sweden. *Energy Research & Social Science*, *10*, 180–191. doi: 10.1016/j.erss.2015.06.014

ISSS of Peking University. (2018). *Chinese Family Panel Studies*. Retrieved from http://www.isss.pku.edu.cn/cfps/EN/

Jalas, M. (2002). A time use perspective on the materials intensity of consumption. *Ecological Economics*, *41*(1), 109–123. doi: 10.1016/s0921-8009(02)00018-6

Jalas, M. (2005). The everyday life context of increasing energy demands: Time use survey data in a decomposition analysis. *Journal of Industrial Ecology*, 9(1–2), 129–145. doi: 10.1162/1088198054084644

Jalas, M. (2009). Time-use rebound effects: An activity-based view of consumption. In H. Herring & S. Sorrell (Eds), *Energy efficiency and sustainable consumption*. London: Palgrave Macmillan.

Jalas, M., & Juntunen, J. K. (2015). Energy intensive lifestyles: Time use, the activity patterns of consumers, and related energy demands in Finland. *Ecological Economics*, 113, 51–59. doi: 10.1016/j.ecolecon.2015.02.016

Karlin, B., Zinger, J. F., & Ford, R. (2015). The effects of feedback on energy conservation: A meta-analysis. *Psychol Bull*, 141(6), 1205–1227. doi: 10.1037/a0039650

Lund, T. B., & Gronow, J. (2014). Destructuration or continuity? The daily rhythm of eating in Denmark, Finland, Norway and Sweden in 1997 and 2012. *Appetite*, 82, 143–153. doi: 10.1016/j.appet.2014.07.004

McKenna, E., Krawczynski, M., & Thomson, M. (2015). Four-state domestic building occupancy model for energy demand simulations. *Energy and Buildings*, 96, 30–39. doi:10.1016/j.enbuild.2015.03.013

Meyer, D., & Bäumer, T. (2020). Less meat, less heat—The potential of social marketing to reduce meat consumption. In Patrick Müller, Patrick Planing, Payam Dehdari, Thomas Bäumer (Eds.), *Innovations for metropolitan areas* (pp. 157–168). Springer Berlin Heidelberg.

National Bureau of Statistics. (2009a). *The 2009 China Statistical Yearbook*. Retrieved from http://www.stats.gov.cn/tjsj/ndsj/2009/indexeh.htm

National Bureau of Statistics. (2009b). *The 2009 Chinese Energy Statistical Yearbook*. China Statistics Press.

National Bureau of Statistics. (2013). *The 2013 China Statistical Yearbook*. Retrieved from http://www.stats.gov.cn/tjsj/ndsj/2013/indexeh.htm

National Bureau of Statistics. (2019a). *The 2019 China Statistical Yearbook*. Retrieved from

National Bureau of Statistics. (2019b). *The 2019 Chinese Energy Statistical Yearbook*. Retrieved from

Newsham, G. R., & Bowker, B. G. (2010). The effect of utility time-varying pricing and load control strategies on residential summer peak electricity use: A review. *Energy Policy*, 38(7), 3289–3296. doi: 10.1016/j.enpol.2010.01.027

Office of Energy Efficiency & Renewable Energy. (2020). *Energy Efficiency Policies and Programs*. Retrieved from https://www.energy.gov/eere/slsc/energy-efficiency-policies-and-programs

Richardson, I., Thomson, M., & Infield, D. (2008). A high-resolution domestic building occupancy model for energy demand simulations. *Energy and Buildings*, 40(8), 1560–1566. doi: 10.1016/j.enbuild.2008.02.006

Richardson, I., Thomson, M., Infield, D., & Clifford, C. (2010). Domestic electricity use: A high-resolution energy demand model. *Energy and Buildings*, 42(10), 1878–1887. doi: 10.1016/j.enbuild.2010.05.023

Swan, L. G., & Ugursal, V. I. (2009). Modeling of end-use energy consumption in the residential sector: A review of modeling techniques. *Renewable and Sustainable Energy Reviews*, *13*(8), 1819–1835. doi: 10.1016/j.rser.2008.09.033

Torriti, J. (2017). Understanding the timing of energy demand through time use data: Time of the day dependence of social practices. *Energy Research & Social Science*, *25*, 37–47. doi: 10.1016/j.erss.2016.12.004

US Energy Information Administration. (1998). *Energy Consumption by End-Use Sector a consumption and supply surveys.*

Vandenbroele, J., Vermeir, I., Geuens, M., Slabbinck, H., & Van Kerckhove, A. (2020). Nudging to get our food choices on a sustainable track. *Proceedings of the Nutrition Society*, *79*(1), 133–146. doi: 10.1017/S0029665119000971

Widén, J., & Wäckelgård, E. (2010). A high-resolution stochastic model of domestic activity patterns and electricity demand. *Applied Energy*, *87*(6), 1880–1892. doi: 10.1016/j.apenergy.2009.11.006

Wiedenhofer, D., Smetschka, B., Akenji, L., Jalas, M., & Haberl, H. (2018). Household time use, carbon footprints, and urban form: A review of the potential contributions of everyday living to the 1.5°C climate target. *Current Opinion in Environmental Sustainability*, *30*, 7–17. doi: 10.1016/j.cosust.2018.02.007

Yao, C., Chen, C., & Li, M. (2012). Analysis of rural residential energy consumption and corresponding carbon emissions in China. *Energy Policy*, *41*, 445–450. doi: 10.1016/j.enpol.2011.11.005

Yu, B., Yang, X., Zhao, Q., & Tan, J. (2020). Causal effect of time-use behavior on residential energy consumption in China. *Ecological Economics*, *175*. doi: 10.1016/j.ecolecon.2020.106706

Zheng, X., Wei, C., Qin, P., Guo, J., Yu, Y., Song, F., & Chen, Z. (2014a). Characteristics of residential energy consumption in China: Findings from a household survey. *Energy Policy*, *75*, 126–135. doi: 10.1016/j.enpol.2014.07.016

Zheng, X., Wei, C., Qin, P., Guo, J., Yu, Y., Song, F., & Chen, Z. (2014b). *Chinese household energy consumption report (2014)*. Beijing: Science Press.

4 Residential CO_2 emissions of lifestyles

4.1 Reconstructing residential CO_2 emissions

With our reconstructed dataset, this chapter examines CO_2 emissions from residential electricity consumption of various lifestyles that are differentiated by time-use patterns. CO_2 emissions that are incurred from daily residential electricity consumption for an activity j by individual i can be calculated with the following equation that combines the results in previous two chapters.

$$C_j^i = T_j^i \cdot CI_j^i = T_j^i \cdot EI_j^i \cdot EF \qquad (4.1)$$

Equation 4.1 CO_2 emissions of activity.

T_j^i : Hours per day for activity j (h/day) for individual i. It not only differs between urban and rural China, but also genuinely refers to individuals as examined in Chapter 2 with those sampled individual residents in the Chinese Time-Use Survey (CTUS). CI_j^i and EI_j^i take average values in urban and rural China, respectively, due to data constraints as analyzed in Chapter 3. EF is the emission factor.

Adding up all CO_2 emissions for daily activities over 24 hours, we can further calculate daily residential CO_2 emissions from electricity consumption:

$$C^i = \sum_j C_j^i \qquad (4.2)$$

Equation 4.2 Daily CO_2 emissions.

DOI: 10.4324/9780429291708-4

4.2 Residential CO_2 emissions by activities

Daily activities correspond to very different contributions of CO_2 emissions from residential electricity consumption, due to their time-use patterns and electricity/CO_2 intensities. In 2018, an average Chinese incurred 1,339 gCO_2/day (Figure 4.1). Unpaid work resulted in 518 gCO_2/day, accounting for 38.7% and being the most among all activities. Personal care & maintenance and watching TV contributed 18.1% and 11.5%, respectively. These three activities occupied 265 minutes or 18.4% of 24 hours (see Chapter 2), but due to their high CO_2 intensity (see Chapter 3), they led to 68.3% of daily CO_2 emissions. Sleeping was also an important activity with 223 gCO_2/day.

For electric appliances with the three operation modes, activity-related appliances accounted for 692 gCO_2/day, being responsible for more than half (51.4%) of total (Figure 4.2). The occupancy-related appliances contributed 553 gCO_2/day, while the background appliances added 94 gCO_2/day. Because different appliances were matched to different appliances, distinct patterns were revealed. Absence from residence had its CO_2 emissions entirely from background appliances (Figure 4.3). CO_2 emissions from Unpaid work and Personal care &

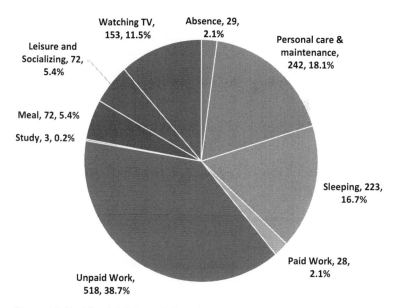

Figure 4.1 Residential CO_2 emissions in 2018 by activity (grams CO_2/person/day).

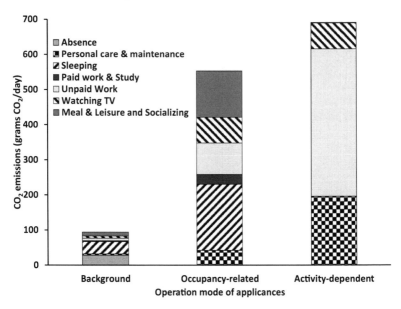

Figure 4.2 CO_2 emissions by activity and operation mode of appliances in 2018.

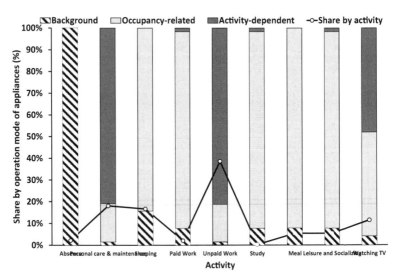

Figure 4.3 Shares of CO_2 emissions by activity and operation mode of appliances in 2018.

maintenance were mainly associated with activity-related appliances due to their active utilization of appliances for performing the activities. Sleeping, paid work, study, meal and leisure & socializing mostly had CO_2 emissions with occupancy-related appliances, mainly to create thermal comfort and brightness. Watching TV required both comfort and TV.

From 2008 to 2018, CO_2 emissions from occupancy-related appliances witnessed the biggest increase, being 119.5%, while those background and activity-related appliances were 40.3% and 41.7% higher, respectively (Figure 4.4). The overall growth was 531.8 gCO_2/day, or 65.9%. It reflects that when China got richer, people started to demand more comfortable living environment with an increasing ownership of such appliances and their usage (Chapter 3). For example, additional CO_2 emissions for watching TV mainly came from occupancy-related appliances, but very minor from activity-related appliances, indicating the much heavier emphasis on comfort. Unpaid work and personal care & maintenance were responsible for almost all growth of CO_2 emissions from activity-related appliances, which should reflect that the Chinese people were using more appliances to make living and household chores more convenient.

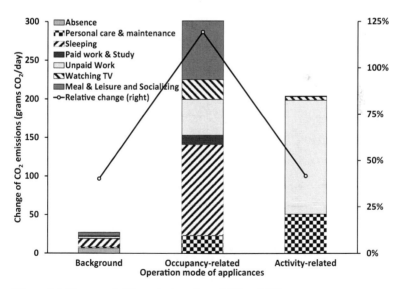

Figure 4.4 Change of CO_2 emissions from 2008 to 2018.

- **Urban and rural lifestyles:**

Urban and rural residence is also more than just a description of the place of individuals living in. It might play an even more influential role for its association with the *hukou* system. It is to indicate the legitimacy of an individual's living in a certain place and attributes to a range of localized personal benefits like land rights, education, housing, medical care, and employment. Its strict separation between urban and rural residents has led to the dualistic economic between urban and rural areas and other social problems. It was only in 2014 that the policy was finally relaxed in most parts of the country and replaced by a unified hukou registration system for urban and rural areas. This relaxation further freed rural residents' geographical mobility and caused an acceleration of urbanization, resulting in a rapid change in residents' lifestyles, which might be also reflected in their residential CO$_2$ emissions.

Urban and rural lifestyles differ significantly in terms of residential CO$_2$ emissions. In 2018, they correspond to 1,240 and 1,497 gCO$_2$/day for a typical resident (Figures 4.5 and 4.6). Unpaid work contributed the most CO$_2$ emissions in both urban and rural lifestyles, being 34.8% and 44.6%, respectively, while Personal care & maintenance were responsible for 24.9% urban emissions but only 9.6% for rural Chinese. Sleeping and watching TV were associated with similar shares of

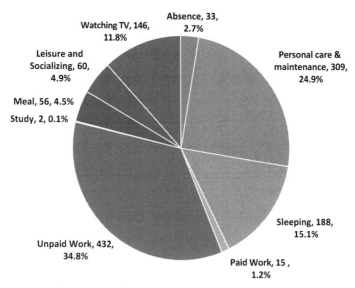

Figure 4.5 Urban residential CO$_2$ emissions in 2018 (grams CO$_2$/day/person).

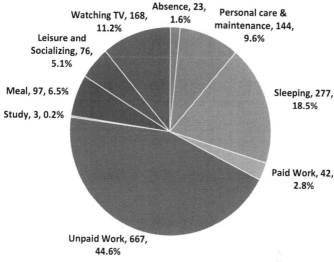

Figure 4.6 Rural residential CO$_2$ emissions in 2018.

residential CO$_2$ emissions across urban and rural lifestyles, being 15.1% and 11.8%, and 18.5% and 11.2%, respectively (Figures 4.5 and 4.6).

Notably in 2018, it was the rural lifestyle that incurred more CO$_2$ emissions from residential electricity consumption. This was in a sharp contrast to the situation in 2008 when the urban lifestyle led to more CO$_2$ emissions (Figure 4.7). In both years, the urban lifestyle emitted significantly more CO$_2$ for personal care & maintenance, primarily from activity-related appliances. Unpaid work in 2018 corresponded to more CO$_2$ emissions in 2018 for an average rural Chinese. Occupancy-related appliances were associated with much more CO$_2$ emissions in the rural lifestyle. These reflect the quick catching up of comfortable living and time-saving electric appliances, which might indicate an eventual reversal of the urban/rural gap. From the perspective of CO$_2$ emissions from residential electricity consumption, accordingly, urbanization may indicate very different directions if projected with 2008 and 2018 results.

Although both rural and urban lifestyles became more carbon intensive, the rural growth rate was much greater than the urban one (Figure 4.8). The biggest increase in both urban and rural lifestyles from 2008 to 2018 was from occupancy-related appliances, being 44.6% and 246.9%, respectively (Figure 4.8). Activity-related appliances witnessed a 16.8% increase of their associated CO$_2$ emissions in the urban lifestyle, and the rate swelled to 72.0% in the rural lifestyle.

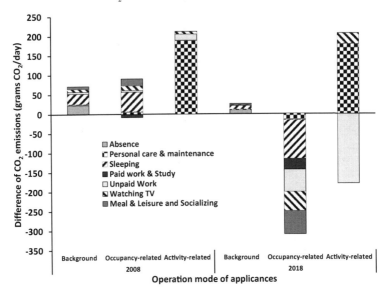

Figure 4.7 Difference of CO$_2$ emissions between urban and rural residents in 2008 and 2018 (negative values indicate that rural Chinese residents correspond to more CO$_2$ emissions).

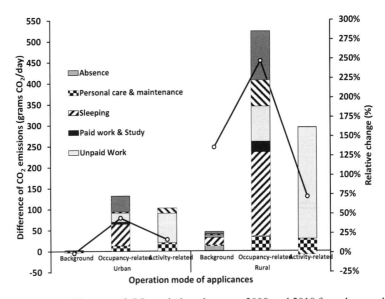

Figure 4.8 Difference of CO$_2$ emissions between 2008 and 2018 for urban and rural residents (negative values indicate that CO$_2$ emissions in 2008 were more than those in 2018).

Background appliances in the urban lifestyle had the least change, being 0.6%, while in the rural lifestyle, it became 135.8% higher. Overall, a typical day of urban and rural Chinese emitted 23.1% and 133.0% more CO$_2$ over the ten years, which illustrates dramatic changes of China's rural lifestyle. This implied that the rural residents in 2018 owned more electric appliances like air conditioners and electric heaters and used them more frequently.

- **Weekday and weekend/holiday lifestyles**

The day of the week, in time-related sociological studies, is often seen as an indicator of how society shapes a person's day through institutional rhythms. It synchronizes and structures the time of day for a group of individuals through the instituted and fixed schedules like work and school (Nicholls & Strengers, 2015). It acts in reproducing the social rhythm, but at the same time, it itself is a socially constructed product. The concept of day of the week is enforced along with the development of industrial society, by alienating people from the family workforce to a factory worker of five days a week.

Although weekdays and weekends/holidays differ significantly in time-use lifestyles (Chapter 2), their CO$_2$ emissions from residential electricity consumption were much less apart from each other (Figure 4.9).

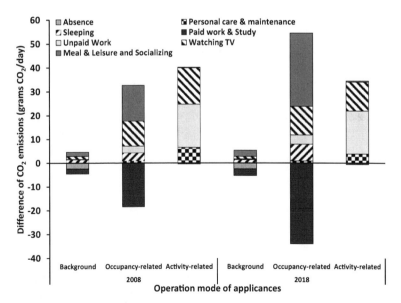

Figure 4.9 Difference of CO$_2$ emissions between weekend and weekday in 2008 and 2018.

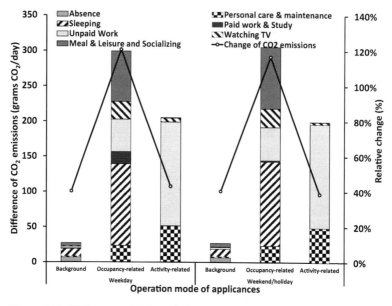

Figure 4.10 Difference of CO_2 emissions between 2008 and 2018 for weekday and weekend/holiday lifestyles.

In 2008, one day during weekends/holidays resulted in 53.9 gCO_2/day more emissions than one day during weekdays. The difference in 2018 was 54.4 gCO_2/day, although significantly more CO_2 emissions were incurred in both categories over the ten years. The impacts of more comfortable living were also reflected when in 2018, occupancy-related appliances accounted for the largest variation between weekends/holidays and weekdays. Over the ten years, weekday and weekend/holiday lifestyles evolved with very similar patterns as CO_2 emissions from appliances at different operation modes increased almost at the same pace (Figure 4.10).

• **Gendered lifestyles**

"Men are breadwinners and women are homemakers." This is a short summary of the traditional Chinese view of the gender division of labor. Men are expected to work and earn money, while women are expected to take care of household chores. However, as China enters modern society, with the economic development of society, the popularization of education, and the emergence of Western egalitarian thinking, the expectations towards gender roles are changing. Women

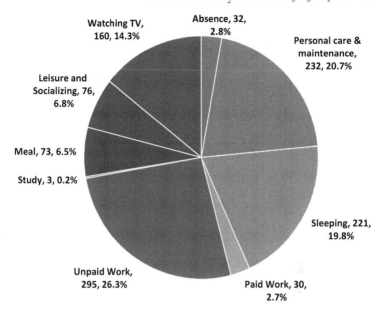

Figure 4.11 Daily residential CO_2 emissions by men in 2018.

are no longer restricted at home, and more of them are involved in employment. Yet, when we look at housework, it is still mainly performed by women (Chapter 2). In other words, women are required to handle both their own paid work and household unpaid work. These groups of women were found to be more likely to incorporate various household appliances such as rice cookers, microwave ovens, and vacuum cleaners in their unpaid work to complete all the required housework in the limited time. And this is also reflected in our reconstructed CO_2 emissions.

The female lifestyle resulted in 424 gCO_2/day more emissions than the male lifestyle in 2018, or 37.8% (Figures 4.11 and 4.12). The gender difference was largely due to a single activity (Figure 4.13). Although unpaid work was responsible for 26.3% of the male lifestyle's CO_2 emissions in 2018 (Figure 4.11), its share in the female lifestyle was much greater at 47.8% (Figure 4.12). An average Chinese woman accordingly had 150.8%, or 444.1 gCO_2/day, more emissions from unpaid work than a man. All other activities together led to 20 gCO_2/day less emissions for the female lifestyle. This stark difference could be further traced to activity-related appliances for performing unpaid work (Figure 4.14).

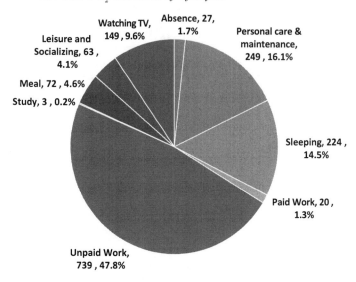

Figure 4.12 Daily residential CO_2 emissions by a typical Chinese woman in 2018.

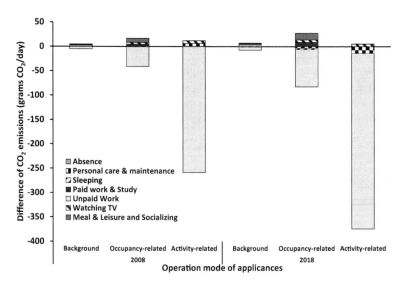

Figure 4.13 Gender differences of residential CO_2 emissions (negative indicates that a woman has more CO_2 emissions).

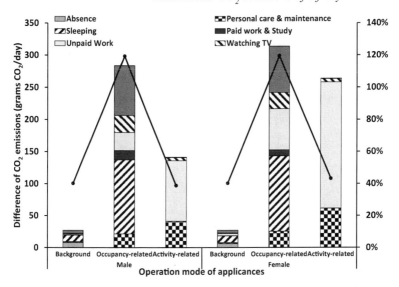

Figure 4.14 Difference of CO_2 emissions between 2008 and 2018 for gendered lifestyles.

• **Aged lifestyles**

Age is another demographic characteristic that we included in the analysis. People often have very distinct lifestyles at different ages. In youth, life focuses often very much on studying and learning, in adulthood on work and family, and in old age on leisure and family. This is also illustrated in their residential CO_2 emissions. The youth lifestyle resulted in 916 gCO₂/day in 2018, while the working-age and retirement lifestyles corresponded to 1,272 and 1,566 gCO₂/day emissions, respectively (Figures 4.15, 4.16 and 4.17). It reflected their distinct time-use patterns (Chapter 2). Study is featured in the youth lifestyle to account for 3.1% of the CO_2 emissions (Figure 4.15). Accordingly, being the activity that accounted for the largest difference (Figure 4.18), unpaid work was associated with 164, 509 and 635 gCO₂/day (17.9%, 40.0% and 40.6% of total), respectively across the three aged lifestyles. Retirement lifestyle features more leisure time with significantly more CO_2 emissions from watching TV. The contrast for leisure and socializing was much smaller. Their different time-use patterns were the key reason because senior citizens spent a greater proportion of their leisure time in watching TV rather than doing other leisure activities, especially on the Internet. It could reflect China's generation gaps. While those three age groups below 45 years old had less CO_2

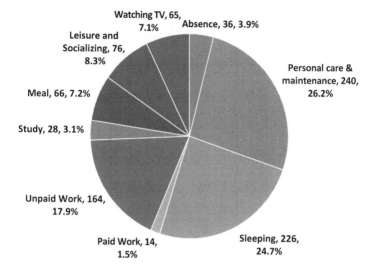

Figure 4.15 Daily residential CO$_2$ emissions by young Chinese (age group: 15–24 years old).

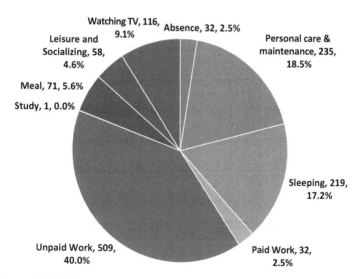

Figure 4.16 Daily residential CO$_2$ emissions by working-age Chinese (age group: 25–54 years old).

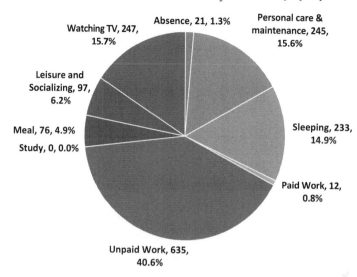

Figure 4.17 Daily residential CO_2 emissions by old Chinese (age group: 65–74 years old).

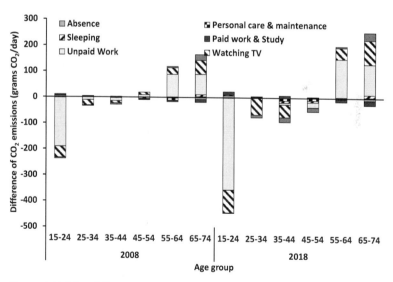

Figure 4.18 The difference of residential CO_2 emissions between individual age groups.

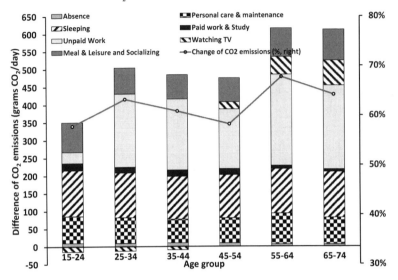

Figure 4.19 The difference of residential CO_2 emissions between 2008 and 2018 by age group.

emissions from watching TV, those three older groups had more (Figure 4.19). These two activities, unpaid work and watching TV, explained most of the differences across aged lifestyles (Figure 4.18).

From 2008 to 2018, residential CO_2 emissions that are associated with aged lifestyles shifted with almost homogeneous proportions, between 57.8% and 67.7% (Figure 4.19). As a result, the difference from the average lifestyle also had relatively stable patterns (Figure 4.18).

• **Lifestyles by education levels**

Education is another crucial social change in China with rapid increase of education levels of an average Chinese and more and more people receiving tertiary education (Chapter 2). Especially in China's economic transformation, education attainment is increasingly considered as one's ticket to certain lifestyle. High-paying jobs such as technology and finance often have high requirements on education levels.

For those with no schooling, activities in a typical day were associated with 1,515 gCO_2 emissions (Figure 4.20), while for those with university education and above, the daily emission level was 1,218 gCO_2 (Figure 4.21). Unpaid work accounted for the largest difference across lifestyles across education levels. Generally, those with less education

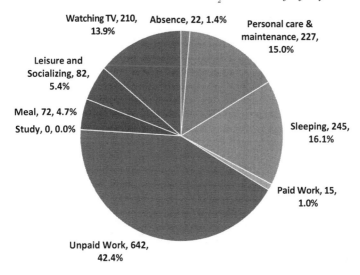

Figure 4.20 Daily residential CO$_2$ emissions by people with no schooling in 2018.

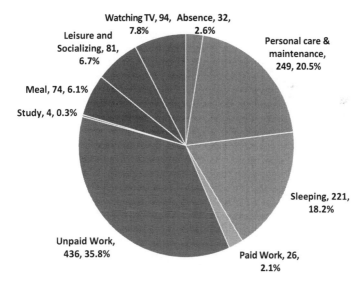

Figure 4.21 Daily residential CO$_2$ emissions by people with university education in 2018.

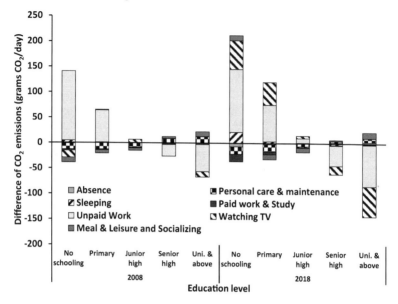

Figure 4.22 The difference of residential CO$_2$ emissions between people with different education levels.

tend to be engaged with more residential CO$_2$ emissions for unpaid work and watching TV, while there was not have much a inter-group difference in other activities (Figure 4.22). Leisure and socializing were associated with about the same amount of residential CO$_2$ emissions for all groups, indicating that residential leisure activities other than watching TV did not present major gaps for people with varying education levels. From 2008 to 2018, all groups showed a significant increase in residential CO$_2$ emissions. Although the growth was more for those with no schooling, the variation was relatively small (Figure 4.23). Watching TV was the most important activity to account for their temporal changes. Lifestyles of lower educational levels tend to have more CO$_2$ emissions from watching TV, while those of university education & above even witnessed a reduction over the ten years (Figure 4.23).

- **Lifestyles by income levels**

Income is a crucial driving factor to determine lifestyles with implications on CO$_2$ emissions. In 2018, those people without income had 1,559 gCO$_2$/day emissions, while those earning 500–1,000 RMB/month and more than 10,000 RMB/month were associated with 1,421 and

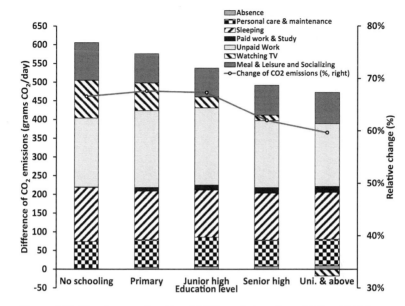

Figure 4.23 The change of residential CO_2 emissions from 2008 to 2018 (negative values indicate that CO_2 emissions in 2008 were more than those in 2018).

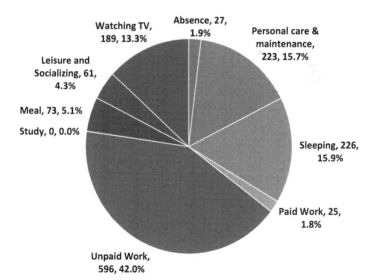

Figure 4.24 Daily residential CO_2 emissions by people with an income between 500 and 1,000RMB/month in 2018.

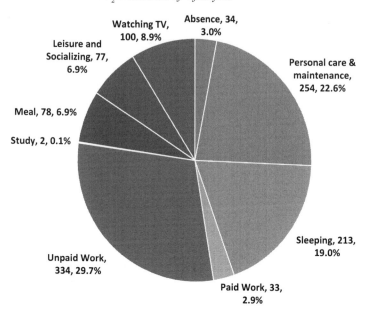

Figure 4.25 Daily residential CO$_2$ emissions by people with an income higher than 10,000RMB/month in 2018.

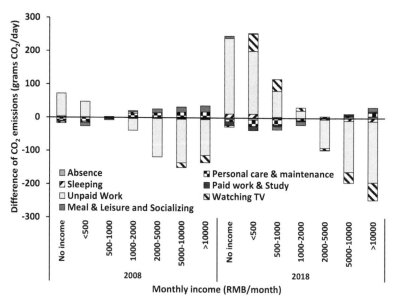

Figure 4.26 Difference of residential CO$_2$ emissions between people with different income levels.

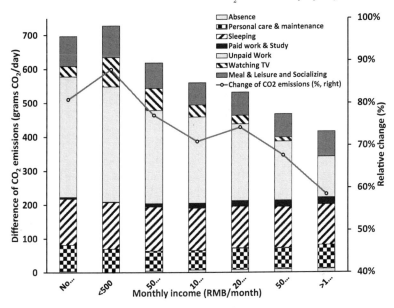

Figure 4.27 Change of residential CO$_2$ emissions from 2008 to 2018.

1,125 gCO$_2$/day (Figures 4.24 and 4.25). Unpaid work accounted for a difference of 262 gCO$_2$/day, out of the overall difference of 297 gCO$_2$/day. Similar to the situation in the lifestyles by education level, the most important activity to determine their residential CO$_2$ emissions is unpaid work (Figure 4.26). As reflected in their household roles and time-use patterns, those with higher education and income levels tend to do less household chores and they also watched less TV in 2018 (Figure 4.26). Over the ten years from 2008 to 2018, all lifestyles by income levels had greater residential CO$_2$ emissions, while those with higher income witnessed smaller growth. Unpaid work and watching TV were responsible for most of the variations across changing lifestyles (Figure 4.27).

4.3 Discussion

Unpaid work, primarily household chores, is the most important component to determine a lifestyle's residential CO$_2$ emissions and especially the difference across lifestyles. This factor is crucial in understanding and explaining this chapter's findings.

The female lifestyle was associated with 37.8% more residential CO$_2$ emissions than the male lifestyle in 2018, and 40.5% more in 2008.

However, this should not be explained as that the female lifestyle is more harmful to the Earth as a more important cause of greenhouse gas emissions and climate change. Instead, the results further reveal gender inequality from the perspective of residential CO_2 emissions. Household chores are generally to serve the entire family, not just the ones who are engaged in the work. Indeed, if excluding unpaid work, the female lifestyle emitted 6.6% and 2.5% less CO_2 per day than the male lifestyle in 2018 and 2008, respectively. It could reflect the double roles of many Chinese women as both income-earners and household chore bearers. Their leisure activities (specifically watching TV and leisure and socializing as in the time-use category) were often squeezed. A more equal gender relationship would entail a more equal loading of unpaid work, which would increase residential CO_2 emissions of the male lifestyle and decrease that of the female lifestyle. Then the gender gap could shrink to result in better quality.

Another lifestyle with a significantly heavier unpaid workload is that of retired people. 23.1% of residential CO_2 emissions resulted from the retirement lifestyle than the working-age lifestyle, and 70.9% more than the youth lifestyle. Similarly, it does not lead to a conclusion that the youth lifestyle is the most climate friendly. Excluding unpaid work, the youth lifestyle was only 1.4% and 19.1% less than the working-age and retirement lifestyles, respectively. Watching TV and leisure and socializing explain a great majority of these remaining differences, with the retirement lifestyle. This result reflects the traditional age-related roles of Chinese multi-generation families: young people are supposed to study hard, while those in the retirement age are expected to help take care of grandchildren and do more household chores when their working-age children are engaged in income-earning jobs. In addition, the retirement lifestyle is indeed more residential and less outdoors.

Although weekend/holiday and weekday lifestyles have visibly different time-use patterns, the time for paid work only increased slightly to result in only 3.1% and 0.3% more overall CO_2 emissions per day in 2008 and 2018, respectively. The difference is much smaller than that within other categories of lifestyles. More holidays will accordingly not have major impacts on China's CO_2 emissions from residential electricity consumption.

Various lifestyles that are analyzed in this chapter are not mutually exclusive but are correlated. For example, education and income levels are closely related as education generally has significant income returns. Older people and especially women tend to receive less education. Although higher education and income levels tend to have less residential CO$_2$ emissions, the trend would become much weaker if excluding unpaid work.

Changing residential CO$_2$ emissions from urban/rural lifestyles reflect both time-use patterns and CO$_2$ intensities. This chapter dissected a prominent reversal of China's urban/rural gap over the ten years. In 2008, an urban Chinese had significantly more residential CO$_2$ emissions, but in 2018, a rural Chinese emitted more. Comfortable living environment witnessed dramatic increase of corresponding CO$_2$ emissions from 2008 to 2018, especially in rural lifestyles. The Chinese people have rapidly improved their living standards together with economic growth. The conventional urban/rural gap as indicated in their residential CO$_2$ emissions is quickly disappearing and gradually reversed.

Developed countries tend to emit much more CO$_2$ per capita than developing countries. Rich people's lifestyle is also very different from poor people. However, this chapter's results showed that the lifestyle of low-income people corresponded to more residential CO$_2$ emissions than that of high-income people. The seemingly counterintuitive result was due to the fact that those with lower income tend to do more household chores with the family and thus have much more CO$_2$ emissions from unpaid work. This mainly reflects the time-use patterns of their lifestyles, which are intertwined with household roles. For example, housewives with no or minimal income do more unpaid work to account for more residential CO$_2$ emissions, while primary breadwinners in the families allocated less time for household chores. Another crucial reason is that our data on CO$_2$ intensity were not able to differentiate among various lifestyles except urban and rural ones, because no energy statistics data are available to the authors to calibrate the reconstructed CO$_2$ intensity. Because this book mainly focuses on the impacts of time-use patterns, this data unavailability issue does not prevent the analysis from achieving the intended research objectives.

Except for urban/rural lifestyles, the analysis in this Chapter primarily reflected the impacts of time-use patterns across various lifestyles and over time. Due to this factor in data unavailability, in comparison with the urban/rural gap, the gender and generation gaps were much more persistent over the years although Chinese society has been going through major multi-faceted transitions.

China's economic transformation has been much faster than the society's evolution pace. For example, although time-use patterns have witnessed much greater changes in China over the ten years from 2008 to 2018 than in developed countries, like in the United States, the CO$_2$

intensities of time-consuming activities skyrocketed with economic growth and much higher household disposable income. More electric appliances have entered ordinary Chinese family homes to create a more comfortable living environment and enhance the time efficiency of completing household chores. Further studies could better differentiate CO$_2$ intensities of activities for various lifestyles.

References

Nicholls, L., & Strengers, Y. (2015). Peak demand and the 'family peak' period in Australia: Understanding practice (in)flexibility in households with children. *Energy Research & Social Science, 9*, 116–124. doi: 10.1016/j.erss.2015.08.018

5 The climate impacts of lifestyles from demographic changes

5.1 China's demographic shifts

This chapter scales up residential CO_2 emissions of different life-styles to the national level for depicting the extent of climate impacts of ongoing changes in demographic profiles and average lifestyles in China.

Urbanization and aging population are found to have microsocial impacts on typical lifestyles, and thus, energy consumption and CO_2 emissions in the residential sector (Wei, Liu, Fan, & Wu, 2007; Zhao, Li, & Ma, 2012). Urbanization is not only a change in geographical location of the inhabitants from rural to urban areas but is also associated with a change in their distribution of their time to activities and of their income to electricity-consuming appliances (Chapters 2 and 3). Aging population is also not just a rise in the proportion of elderly population, but in China, it is also a shift in the typical lifestyles to a more leisurely and family oriented one (Chapter 4). We examine and discuss the extent of the potential impacts of these two demographic changes on residential CO_2 emissions in China in the perspective of lifestyle. In addition, we will discuss the current situation of urbanization and aging population in China to provide better contextual information to the reader.

Time-use measures will also be explored on to what extent these alternative measures can serve climate mitigation. Two analyses will be conducted for the purpose. One is decomposition analysis, that disaggregates the difference in residential CO_2 emissions between 2008 and 2018 into the impacts of time-use patterns and the CO_2 intensity of activities, to provide a basic quantification of lifestyle climate impacts, particularly in a time-use perspective. The other is sensitivity analysis

DOI: 10.4324/9780429291708-5

used for examining the range of CO_2 emission reduction that can be actualized by time-use measures like encouraging low carbon-intensive outdoor activities.

Over the past three decades, China has experienced tremendous demographic changes. Its economic structure, population geographic distribution, and lifestyle have been greatly altered. And two of the most notable and often discussed are urbanization and the aging population.

• Urbanization

Since the economic open-door policy of the late 1970s, the urbanization process has advanced rapidly in China. Millions of rural residents have been attracted to move into cities for their higher-income job opportunities and better social supports. The urban proportion of the total population has increased rapidly, from 17.9% in 1978 to 48% in 2008 and 59.6% in 2018 (Figure 5.1). In just four decades, the composition of Chinese population has reversed dramatically, with the number of urban residents far exceeding the number of rural residents. However, along with rapid urbanization, the carbon emission level in China has also been growing quickly, causing various environmental, ecological and climate issues. The current urbanization rate in China

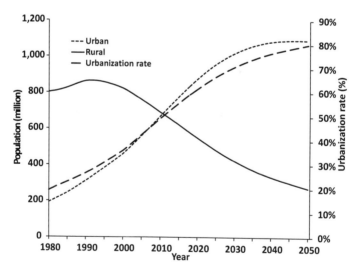

Figure 5.1 Urban, rural population and urbanization rate in China.
(United Nations, 2019).

remains lower, however, than the typical urbanization rate of 78% in developed countries. Continuous growth in urbanization in China may be expected.

On the other hand some research literature suggests that urbanization does not necessarily bring about an increase in CO_2 emissions. It appears that the agglomeration effect brought by dense urban populations can allow more efficient utilization of resources, thereby reducing CO_2 emissions. The well-known Environmental Kuznets Curve effect—describing an inverted U-shape relationship between urbanization and environmental pollution—can also be applied to CO_2, which when economic development reaches a certain level, with an increase in per-capita income, knowledge levels and environmental awareness, CO_2 emissions gradually decline. Such a relationship may also be reflected in individual lifestyles, so that between 2008 and 2018 CO_2 emissions by urban residents increased at a slower rate than those of rural residents (Chapter 4).

• Aging population

Aging population is another rapid and alarming demographic change in China. Between 1990 and 2019, the population aged 65 or above grew at an average annual rate of 3.6 million people. As of the end of 2019, the Chinese elderly population has reached 166 millions, with an aging rate of 11.9%, surpassing the total elderly population in Europe, making China the country with the largest elderly population at present. During the same period, the dependency ratio has risen from 8.3% in 1990 to 16.8% in 2019 (Figure 5.2). It is also expected that by 2030, with the aging of baby boomers born between the 1960s and the mid-1970s, the aging rate of Chinese will reach 25%; and that China will become an aged society.

The relationship between changes in age structure of the population and CO_2 emissions has been examined in a number of studies, examining the impacts on carbon emissions of factors like the proportion of elderly population and the age of the labor force. Most of the studies showed that there was a positive relationship between the two. It is argued that it is because the elderly tend to have higher usage of fossil fuels than the younger generation. Yet, in some recent studies of carbon emission modeling in China argued that the relationship of aging population and carbon emission is also not linear, but in a U shape, namely CO_2 emissions increase at the beginning of population aging and decrease after a certain level of population aging.

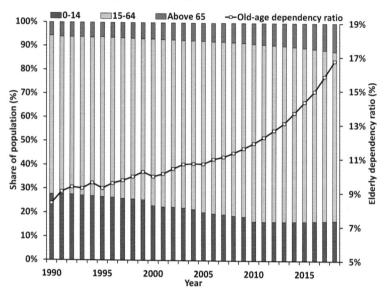

Figure 5.2 Age composition and elderly dependency ratio (above 65 vs 15–64 years old) in China, from 1990–2018.

(National Bureau of Statistics, 2019).

5.2 Climate impacts of the major ongoing demographic shifts in China

This section will first examine the microsocial impacts of urbanization and aging population on typical time-use lifestyles in China, and then discuss their impacts on residential CO_2 emission. Typical lifestyles and corresponding emission levels are projected from a time-use perspective. That is, the impacts of the two demographic changes on the average activities time spent and residential CO_2 emissions of Chinese residents are isolated and estimated by assuming a constant CO_2 intensity of activities. Estimates are based on four data items: (i) time spent on activities (Chapter 2) and (ii) CO_2 intensities of activities (Chapter 3) from this book, and (iii) projected Chinese urbanization rate or age distribution, and (iv) projected total Chinese population from United Nations' World Population Prospect (United Nations, 2019). The time span of the study is from 2008 to 2050. Because CO_2 intensities and emission factor of electricity in the future are very much uncertain and they are not the primary focus of this book, our estimation fixes them at the 2018 level and only considers time-use-defined lifestyles in projecting future residential CO_2 emissions from electricity consumption.

- Urbanization

China is expected to continue to experience rapid urbanization over the next 30 years. In 2050, it will rise to 80%, with 1,091 million urban population (Figure 5.3). The typical lifestyle will become more leisurely-focused, but less work-oriented under both 2008 and 2018 time-use lifestyles (Figure 5.4). The share of time spent on leisure and socializing is considerably higher in 2050 than 2018, ranging from 11% under the 2008 time-use lifestyle to a slightly smaller 4% under the 2018 lifestyle. Similarly, for paid work, the reduction under the 2008 lifestyle was 19%, much larger than the 13% under the 2018 lifestyle. Meanwhile, the changes in the other seven activities were much less pronounced, all below 5%.

The annual residential CO_2 emission exhibited an inverted U-shape for both the 2008 and 2018 time-use lifestyle (Figure 5.3). Emission levels increased continuously and peaked at 679.4 million tons in 2025 for the 2008 time-use lifestyle and 703.2 million tons in 2023 for the 2018 time-use lifestyle, then gradually declined. In 2050, the projected

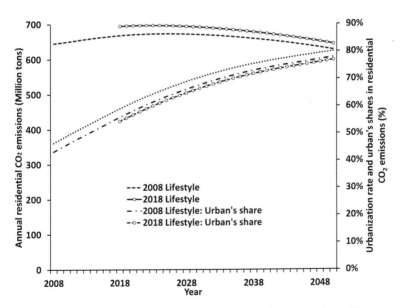

Figure 5.3 Residential CO_2 emissions from electricity generation with projected urbanization rates (2008–2050).

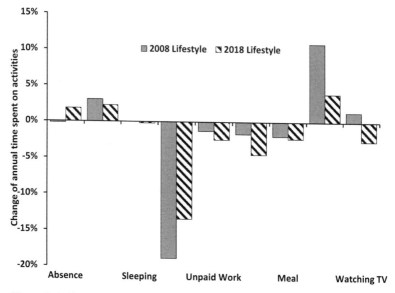

Figure 5.4 Changes of average time spent by activities in China from 2018 to 2050 with projected urbanization rates, following the 2008 and 2018 time-use lifestyles.

emission levels were 632.5 million tons and 648.8 million tons, respectively, for the two time-use lifestyles. These resembled the Environmental Kuznets Curve effect, but here it was not as a result of improvement in environmental awareness and income, but as a consequence of the interactions of time-use lifestyles, population, and the urbanization rate.

Interestingly, when the changes of annual residential CO_2 emission were dissected into activity level, it exhibited a completely different picture than that in the average time spent on activities (Figure 5.5). There was no outstanding difference in leisure and socializing from 2018 to 2050, only a 1% decrease under the 2008 time-use lifestyle and even an 8% decrease under the 2018 time-use lifestyle. But for personal care and maintenance—the most CO_2-intensive activity reported in Chapter 3, the rise was much more significant, at 11% and 10% under the 2008 and 2018 time-use lifestyle, respectively. For paid work, the reduction in residential CO_2 emission remains relatively high, as did the average time spent, at 29% and 25% of the two time-use lifestyles, respectively. Emissions contributed by other activities were more variable, ranging from −2% to 11%.

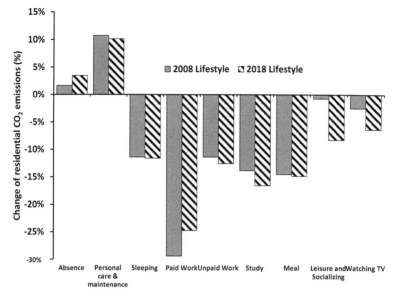

Figure 5.5 Change of annual residential CO_2 emissions from electricity consumption with projected urbanization rates between 2018 and 2050, following the 2008 and 2018 time-use lifestyles.

• Aging population

Aging is also expected to be vital in the coming 30 years in China. The proportion of elderly population aged 55–74 and 75 or above will rise from 15.5% and 2.8% in 2010 to at 27.1% and 14.1% in 2050 (Figure 5.6). The typical lifestyle will shift towards to elderly lifestyle which was more leisure and family-oriented than other age groups (Chapter 4). In 2050, the typical shares of time spent of those aged 15 to 74 on leisure and socializing and watching television were much higher in 2050 than 2020, rising by 6% and 5% under the 2008 time-use lifestyle, respectively, and by 4% and 9% under the 2018 time-use lifestyle, respectively. A relatively high rise was also found in unpaid work, at 4% under both two time-use lifestyles, respectively. In contrast, reductions in average time-spent were found in absence (3%; 4%) and paid work (6%; 6%) indicating that less time on average will be spent outside the residence (Figure 5.9).

The annual residential CO_2 emission with projected age profile from 15 to 74 also exhibited the same inverted U-shape as urbanization for both the 2008 and 2018 time-use lifestyle, but with a much smaller magnitude (Figure 5.7). Emission levels increased continuously and

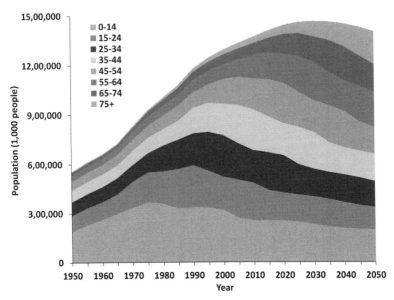

Figure 5.6 Population by age groups.
(United Nations, 2019).

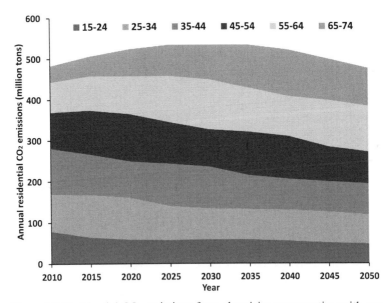

Figure 5.7 Residential CO$_2$ emissions from electricity consumption with projected age profiles from 15 to 74 years old, following 2008 time-use
lifestyle.

peaked at 533.8 million tons in 2025 for the 2008 time-use lifestyle and 544.7 million tons in 2030 for the 2018 time-use lifestyle, followed by a more rapid decline due to shrinking population in those age groups between 15 and 74 years old (Figure 5.6), not the aging profile. In 2050, the projected emission levels were 476.0 million tons and 486.5 million tons, respectively, for the two time-use lifestyles. The retirement lifestyle for those above 65 years old and especially those above 75 is expected to play an increasingly important role in determining China's overall residential CO_2 emissions.

For the activity-level changes of annual residential CO_2 emission, its distribution was roughly similar to the one in average time spent, but the magnitude of change was much higher for some activities and smaller for the others (Figure 5.10). Personal care and maintenance and study were reported to have more profound fluctuations, by 14% and 18% under the 2008 time-use lifestyle and 8% and 34% under the 2018 time-use lifestyle. In contrast, activities like leisure and socializing, watching television and unpaid work had much smaller changes (Figure 5.8).

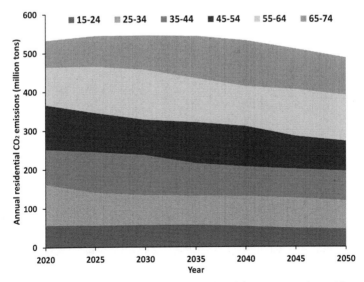

Figure 5.8 Residential CO_2 emissions from electricity consumption with projected age profiles from 15 to 74 years old, following 2018 time-use lifestyle.

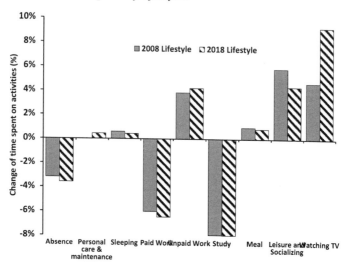

Figure 5.9 Change of average time spent by activities in China from 2020 to 2050 with projected age profiles from age 15 to 74 years old, following the 2008 and 2018 time-use lifestyles.

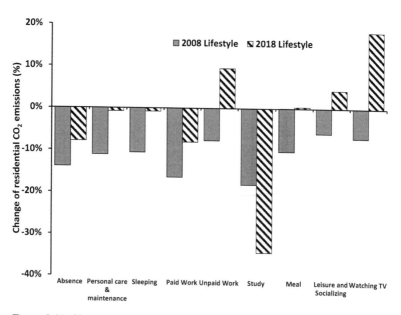

Figure 5.10 Change of residential CO_2 emissions from electricity consumption with projected age profiles from age 15 to 74 between 2020 and 2050, following the 2008 and 2018 time-use lifestyles.

5.3 Climate impacts of time-use patterns

Decomposition analysis is performed to disaggregate the difference in residential CO_2 emission between 2008 and 2018 into the impacts of time-use pattern and CO_2 intensity of activities, to provide a basic quantification of lifestyle climate impacts. Among all the existing decomposition analysis method, the additive LMDI decomposition analysis is selected to perform, as it is the existing most preferrable decomposition method, that is easy to interpret, leaves no residuals, and offers satisfaction for the reversal test (e.g., Ang, 2004; Nie & Kemp, 2014; Zang, Zhao, Wang, & Guo, 2017). It applies to decompose the difference in residential CO_2 emission between typical 2008 and 2018 Chinese time-use (the amount of time spent on each activity) and CO_2 intensity effect (the amount of CO_2 emission per person per hour of an activity). In calculation, the impacts of each factor are calculated based on the principle of letting the factor shift to the level of urban resident, while the alternative factor remains at the level of rural resident. And it is the sum of the respective effects in all eight activity categories (denoted as subscript i). Note that in order to isolate the impacts of lifestyle factors, population changes between 2008 and 2018 is excluded here.

Result of decomposition analysis showed that majority of the variations in residential CO_2 emission between 2008 and 2018 was due to CO_2 intensity effect, which contributed for 94.6% of the total difference (Figure 5.11). By activity category, the highest CO_2 intensity effects were found for unpaid work, sleeping, and watching television, accounting for 34%, 21% and 13% of the total variation, respectively. All three of these activities were the most time spent activities (Chapter 2). Besides, the high CO_2 intensive activity, personal care and maintenance, was found to have a considerable high CO_2 intensity effect of 11%. By appliance operation mode, a similar high share of CO_2 intensity effect was found in occupancy-related and activity-related CO_2 emission, 51.9% and 41.7%, respectively, but only 6.4% in background CO_2 emission (Figure 5.12).

Time-use effect accounted for 5.4% of total variations in CO_2 emission (Figure 5.11). By activity, the biggest time-use effect was the negative effect in watching television, which accounted for −4.1% of the total change (Figure 5.11). In addition, relatively high positive time-use effects were found in personal care & maintenance, unpaid work and leisure and socializing, at 3.6%, 3.9% and 2.1%, respectively. By appliance operation mode, the time-use effect was primarily reflected in activity-related CO_2 emission, which accounted for 77.2% of the

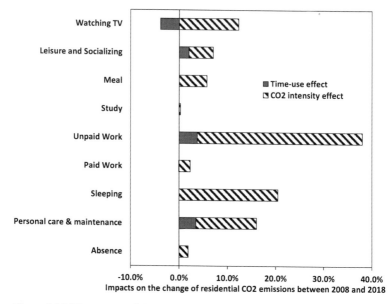

Figure 5.11 Time use and CO_2 intensity effects on the differences of residential CO_2 emissions in 2008 and 2018 by activities.

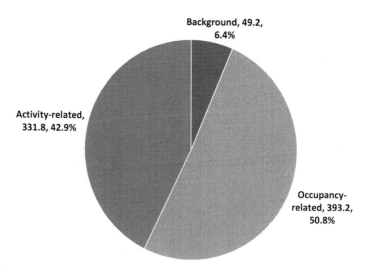

Figure 5.12 CO_2 intensity effects on the differences of residential CO_2 emissions (million tons; % of total) from electricity consumption between 2008 and 2018, by appliance operation mode.

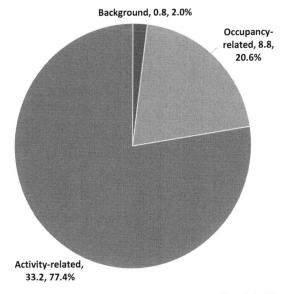

Figure 5.13 Time-use effects on the differences in residential CO_2 emissions (million tons; % of total) from electricity consumption between 2008 and 2018 by appliance operation mode.

total changes (Figure 5.13). Its effects in occupancy-related and background CO_2 emission were much smaller, 20.9% and 2.0%. However, this does not mean that the climate impact of time-use pattern could be ignored. Considering the annual Chinese residential CO_2 emission, this 5% time-use effect could be converted into more than 35 million tons of CO_2 emission, which is higher than total CO_2 emission of countries like Switzerland, Norway, and Sweden (World Bank, 2020).

5.4 Climate impacts of time-use management

Time-use management can be designed and implemented as an alternative pathway to climate mitigation. In this section, a sensitivity analysis was conducted to examine the range of CO_2 emission that could be achieved by encouraging residents to participate in an additional hour of low carbon-intensive outdoor activities per day. In calculation, it is assumed that this hour is reallocated proportionally from activities other than sleeping. The reallocated time spent on activities are then multiplied by the CO_2 intensity reconstructed in Chapter 3 to estimate the CO_2 reduction from the original emission level.

By encouraging residents in participating an additional hour in low carbon-intensive outdoor activities per day, it can bring about a considerable reduction in residential CO_2 emission, which amounted to 32.5 million tons CO_2/year in 2008 and 70.2 million tons CO_2/year in 2018, respectively (Figure 5.14). This is equivalent to mitigate the total annual CO_2 emission of some European countries like Greece (65.3 million tons CO_2/year), Austria (63.2 million tons CO_2/year), Switzerland (37.5 million tons CO_2/year), Norway (37.4 million tons CO_2/year), and Sweden (36.0 million tons CO_2/year). In terms of appliance operation mode, activity-related appliances have a share of 73% and 65% share of the annual CO_2 reduction in 2008 and 2018, respectively, higher than the 27% and 35% of the occupancy-related (Figure 5.14). As for the background appliances, there is no reduction because their operation and energy consumption are not influenced by the occupancy nor activity of the residents.

Due to the differences in the share of time spent, CO_2 intensity and CO_2 composition of the activities, each activity exhibits its distinct CO_2 reduction. In 2008, the biggest reduction is in unpaid work, at 47.0%, followed by personal care and maintenance and watching television, at 25.4% and 16.6%, respectively (Figure 5.15). The reductions

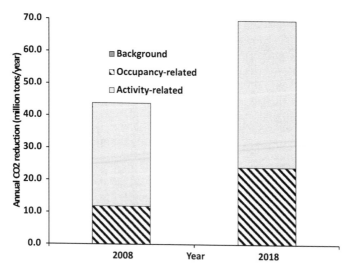

Figure 5.14 Reductions of residential CO_2 emissions from electricity consumption by appliance operation modes with one more hour more per day doing outdoor activities in 2008 and 2018.

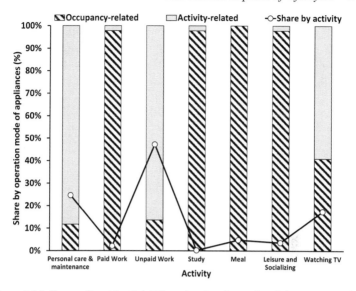

Figure 5.15 Share of residential CO$_2$ reduction from electricity consumption by activity and appliance operation mode with an additional hour per day doing outdoor activities in 2008.

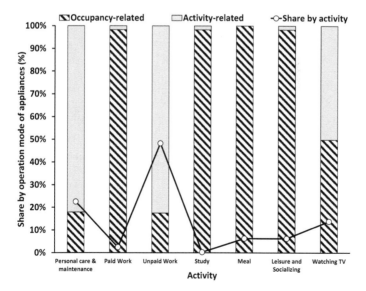

Figure 5.16 Share of residential CO$_2$ reduction from electricity consumption by activity and appliance operation mode with an additional hour per day doing outdoor activities in 2018.

of all these three activities are primarily in activity-related emission, at 86%, 89%, and 59%, respectively. Other four in-residence activities together account for only 5.1% of the emission reductions; and they are mainly occupancy-related emission. In 2018, the distribution is fairly the same, with a slight increase in CO_2 reductions from unpaid work by 1%, but a slight decrease from personal care and maintenance and watching television by −3.1% and −2.2%, respectively (Figure 5.16).

References

Ang, B. W. (2004). Decomposition analysis for policymaking in energy. *Energy Policy*, *32*(9), 1131–1139. doi: 10.1016/s0301-4215(03)00076-4

National Bureau of Statistics. (2019). *The 2019 China Statistical Yearbook*. Retrieved from

Nie, H., & Kemp, R. (2014). Index decomposition analysis of residential energy consumption in China: 2002–2010. *Applied Energy*, *121*, 10–19. doi: 10.1016/j.apenergy.2014.01.070

United Nations. (2019). *The 2019 Revision of World Population Prospects*. Retrieved from https://population.un.org/wpp/

Wei, Y., Liu, L., Fan, Y., & Wu, G. (2007). The impact of lifestyle on energy use and CO_2 emission: An empirical analysis of China's residents. *Energy Policy*, *35*(1), 247–257. doi: 10.1016/j.enpol.2005.11.020

World Bank. (2020). *CO_2 Emissions (kt)*. Retrieved from https://data.worldbank.org/indicator/EN.ATM.CO2E.KT

Zang, X., Zhao, T., Wang, J., & Guo, F. (2017). The effects of urbanization and household-related factors on residential direct CO_2 emissions in Shanxi, China from 1995 to 2014: A decomposition analysis. *Atmospheric Pollution Research*, *8*(2), 297–309. doi: 10.1016/j.apr.2016.10.001

Zhao, X., Li, N., & Ma, C. (2012). Residential energy consumption in urban China: A decomposition analysis. *Energy Policy*, *41*, 644–653. doi: 10.1016/j.enpol.2011.11.027

6 Time-use management for carbon mitigation

6.1 Time use and residential CO_2 emissions

China's climate goals have aroused intense discussion on the complex relationships between the society and CO_2 emissions. This study proposes a time-use perspective to quantitatively illustrate lifestyles and explore related CO_2 emissions from residential electricity consumption.

The changes in everyday lifestyle between 2008 and 2018 were reviewed by analyzing time-use data collected in the CTUS 2008 and 2018. The time-use patterns of people with different socio-economic features were examined to sketch the evolutions of their daily life over the decade with rapid social changes and economic development in China. Significant evolution was found in all studied lifestyles with respects to weekday and weekdays, urban and rural, gender, age, education level and income level.

Furthermore, we devised and applied a bottom-up approach to construct direct residential electricity and CO_2 intensities of activities (Wh/hour/person and grams CO_2/hour/person). Activities and electric appliances were first reclassified into three occupancy states (background, occupancy related, and activity related) based on the nature of their functions, and then they were further matched. The electricity intensity is calculated from electric appliance characteristics (ownership, power rate and usage) and sharing characteristics (number of household members involved in activities). CO_2 intensity is further calculated, considering CO_2 emission factor of electricity. Personal care and maintenance, unpaid work, and watching TV were found to have the highest electricity and CO_2 intensities. They use specific appliances (e.g., electric water heater, washing machine, and television) during the activity.

Combining time-use patterns and residential CO_2 intensity, we quantified the CO_2 emissions of residential electricity consumption for

DOI: 10.4324/9780429291708-6

various lifestyles. Unpaid work, primarily household chores, played the most crucial role in determining residential CO_2 emissions of various lifestyles. As a result, women and retirement lifestyles corresponded to more residential CO_2 emissions. Because household chores are conducted for the entire family, this result should not be explained that these lifestyles have greater climate impacts. Over the years, more electric appliances have entered ordinary Chinese families to create more comfortable living environment and enhance the time efficiency of completing household chores.

We continued exploring how time-use patterns and demographic changes affect China's overall CO_2 emissions from residential electricity consumption. Shifting Chinese time-use pattern to a low-CO_2-intensive one is crucial, especially with the ongoing demographic changes like urbanization and aging population. For example, if an average Chinese spends one more hour in outdoor activities per day, it can bring about a considerable reduction in residential CO_2 emission, being 32.5 and 70.2 million tons CO_2/year, corresponding to 2008 and 2018 lifestyles, respectively. This is equivalent to the total annual CO_2 emissions of countries such as Greece, Austria, Switzerland, Norway or Sweden.

This study has not covered all residential energy consumption but only focused on residential electricity consumption. In 2018, besides 1,005.9 TWh of electricity, China's residential sector also directly consumed 77.1 million tons of coal, 73.3 million tons of oil products, 46.8 billion m^3 of natural gas, and 1,216.8 PJ of heat (National Bureau of Statistics, 2019). These mostly carbon-based fuels were also consumed for conducting time-use activities. In 2018, electricity accounted for 52.4% of all CO_2 emissions from energy consumption in China's residential sector, or 684.6 million tons, being the largest source of CO_2 emissions (Figure 6.1). In comparison, entire Germany emitted 734.4 million tons in the same year (BP, 2021). Electricity's share was 50.3% in 2008, only slightly smaller than that in 2018 (Figures 6.1 and 6.2). China's residential energy consumption has been cleaner especially with coal's importance declining rapidly, from 25.2% in 2008 to 12.8% in 2018. Its absolute contribution was also smaller, from 197.8 million tons CO_2 to 166.7 million tons. Natural gas, in contrast, has been actively replacing coal in households with its share climbing significantly. Due to much higher ownership of private vehicles and greater mobility, oil witnessed the largest increase of the relative and absolute contributions. Its CO_2 emissions more than doubled during the ten years from 89.9 million tons CO_2 to 226.0 million tons. The time use

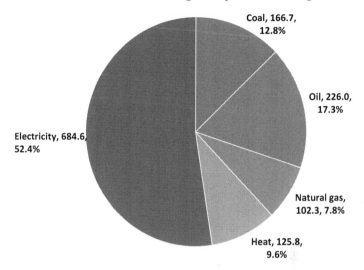

Figure 6.1 CO_2 emissions from the residential sector by fuel in 2008.

(Emission factors are from IPCC (IPCC, 2006). Global Warming Potential values for CO_2, CH_4 and N_2O are from IPCC AR5 (IPCC, 2013).

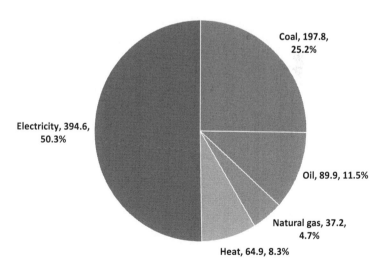

Figure 6.2 CO_2 emissions from the residential sector by fuel in 2018.

for transportation is significantly related to oil consumption and associate CO_2 emissions. Further studies could consider CO_2 emissions from these fuels in understanding how time-use patterns shape residential CO_2 emissions.

6.2 Shaping climate-friendly time-use patterns

Time-use patterns can be greatly shaped by policies and local living environment. The prolonged COVID-19 pandemic has had profound impacts on all aspects of people's lives worldwide, with more than 248 million infections and five million deaths as of November 5, 2021 (WHO, 2021). As an effort to slow the spread of COVID-19, lockdowns and stay-at-home orders were implemented. This in turn significantly changed time-use lifestyles (Sullivan et al., 2021). In China, residents' activities were also observed to shift from outside to at the residences during the lockdown and other social constraints during the pandemic (Yao & Zhang, 2021). Average outdoor time decreased by 40% compared to pre-pandemic period. Time spent on activities was also found to vary significantly, with more time spent on unpaid work (nine minutes more on weekdays; 91 minutes more on weekends/holidays) and less on travel (30 minutes less on weekdays; 70 minutes less on weekends/holidays) and shopping (3.3 minutes less on weekdays; 22.9 minutes less on weekends/holidays).

During lockdown, residential electricity consumption has increased dramatically by up at 30%, as activities at home increase, such as teleworking, steaming and entertaining, online shopping—and they were all powered by electricity (Chen, Zarazua de Rubens, Xu, & Li, 2020; Krarti & Aldubyan, 2021). A study on residential electricity consumption in Texas reported an increase in net electricity consumption (Krarti & Aldubyan, 2021). By end-use consumption, the HVAC electricity use increased by 25% in April 2020 over the 2017 to 2019 average; the non-HVAC electricity consumption increased by 16%, with refrigerator, consuming an average of 12% more due to the higher frequency of door openings and closings throughout the day. While household energy consumption has an overall increase, the more significant changes was in the shape of load profiles. Working-from-home eliminates the need for communing and preparation for work, deriving a delayed and smaller morning peak load to the typical working hours, i.e., 09:00 (Krarti & Aldubyan, 2021).

Nudge—a gentle push to people towards behavioral changes—is an established concept in behavioral economics. In this sub-discipline of economics, it emphasizes that humans are not always irrational, and that their behaviors are often bounded by cognitive biases. Our decisions are often not the best due to the biases derived from frames of choice (Daniel Kahneman & Tversky, 1979), inertia (Samuelson & Zeckhauser, 1988), and limitations of knowledge and computational power (Kahneman, 2003; Simon, 1972). Therefore, to guide people to the right behavior, the key job of policymakers and experts is suggested to be architecting choices, removing possible biases, and making the choice environment simpler, clearer, and more capable to drive people to make the best decisions for themselves and for common goods (Ariely, 2008, 2011). In most of time, our decision is meanwhile driven by intuition and diverted from the best decisions that more likely to be derived from conscious thought. A range of measures were therefore developed under the concept of nudge to optimize the choice environment (Sunstein, 2014; Thaler & Sunstein, 2008). The ten typical measures—default rules, simplification, social norming, facilitation, disclosure, warning, commitment, reminder, elicitation, and consequence information—have been used with some degree of success in fields like health, education, and finance (Damgaard & Nielsen, 2018; DeBondt, Forbes, Hamalainen, & Gulnur Muradoglu, 2010; Vallgarda, 2012). It, or more often called "green nudging", has also been used for environmental issues such as energy use (Darby, 2010; Delmas, Fischlein, & Asensio, 2013; Fischer, 2008), food (Demarque, Charalambides, Hilton, & Waroquier, 2015; Vandenbroele, Vermeir, Geuens, Slabbinck, & Van Kerckhove, 2020), and transportation (Byerly et al., 2018; Nielsen et al., 2017) to push people to engage in green and stop wasteful behaviors.

Another concept in discussing behavioral changes is social practice theories. They differ than behavioral economics, psychology, and other behavior-related disciplines, constructing a distinctive social ontology. They view that the world is constructed and ordered by social practices—the routinized and habitual activities performed in day-to-day basis, rather than individuals and their attitudes, behaviors, or choices (Strengers, 2012). In other words, they suggest that to change a behavior, it should not aim at influencing individuals, as they are only the carriers of the practices. The target should be the practice itself and its constituted elements. Though there is slight difference in the definition of these elements, the common elements include (i) common understanding that the meaning and value of the practice, (ii) rules that procedures and protocols adhered to the practice, (iii) practical knowledge that the know-how in carrying out the practice, and (iv) material infrastructure that physical items required for the practice to be performed. These elements produce, remain, and adjust the practice through their interactions with each other (Shove, Pamtzar, & Watson, 2012). And since the 2010s, these theories have been often applied to discuss how to change the level of energy intensity (Anderson, 2016; Shove, 2003, 2010; Shove et al., 2012; Shove, Trentmann, & Wilk, 2009; Shove, Walker, Tyfield, & Urry, 2014), and the timing of practices (Nicholls & Strengers, 2015; Strengers, 2012; Torriti, Hanna, Anderson, Yeboah, & Druckman, 2015).

Both theories suggest that structuring physical environments is essential to facilitate the shift to less energy-intensive activities (Costa & Kahn, 2013; Strengers & Maller, 2011). Using the example of a transport modal shift from private cares and bicycles, behavioral scientists Pucher and Buehler (2008) pointed out that the provision of a bicycle-friendly environment was the key to the successful experiences of Denmark, Germany, and the Netherlands. Bicycles and related infrastructure, such as separate bicycle lanes along heavily travelled roads and intersections, traffic calming measures (e.g., signing and speed bumps) in residential areas, and extensive bicycle parking, have been cycling safe and convenient, encouraging more demographic groups, including children, seniors, and women, to participate in this transport modal shift. In addition, well-designed bicycle routes with good connections to practical origins and destinations such as public transportation, schools, offices, and shopping areas also enable bicycle use to expand from recreational purposes to daily transportation. Nevertheless, practice theorists emphasized that the provision of physical infrastructure alone is not sufficient to sustain the environmentally friendly behavioral change; it needs to be coupled with two other elements of practice, namely, meaning and practical knowledge. Returning to our example of promoting bicycles as a means of everyday transport, Larsen (2016) suggested the sustained success of the transport model shift in Copenhagen stemmed not only from the availability of cycling infrastructure (materials), but also from its constellation with the good cultural meaning of cycling (meanings) and citizens' ability to cycle (practical knowledge)—and this was not to be achieved by government alone, but with the cooperation of citizens. The Copenhagen's government provided a bicycle-friendly physical environment, as well as actively promoting the positive aspects of cycling, such as its environmental benefits as a pathway to a healthier and more enjoyable city. On the other hand, Copenhageners helped to normalize bicycle usage by giving it modish meanings and developing related practical knowledge. Cycling in their perception represented freedom, speed and flexibility, namely, daily travelling with bicycling rarely encounter traffic jams, are easy to park and are able to take shortcuts. In addition, they also mastered the daily use of bicycles, such as finding shortcuts, fly-parking, and light locking. All of these have made cycling the fastest and the coolest transport option in Copenhagen, sustaining transport modal shift to cycling.

These theoretical and empirical studies provide a ground for what measures could be taken to shift individuals' time use from CO_2-intensive activities and reallocate them to less intensive ones, so as to reduce the Chinese residential CO_2 emissions in the time-use perspective. They proved that time-use patterns could be more actively managed as a contributing means for mitigating China's overall residential CO_2 emissions and further for providing a building block to achieve China's daunting carbon goals, i.e., peak CO_2 emissions by 2030 and carbon neutrality by 2060.

In our study, it is found that most CO_2 emissions from residential electricity consumption are associated with occupancy and activity-related electric appliances. For inducing residents to voluntarily reduce such residential CO_2 emissions, one clear direction in time perspective is to encourage the participation in low-CO_2-intensive outdoor activities. To facilitate this shift, it needs to be achieved through changes in the three elements of practices: urban planning, community, and group activities. First, on the urban planning side, constructing public recreational spaces in close proximity to homes, such as urban parks and squares, is necessary to make outdoor low-CO_2-intensive recreation like square dancing an attractive and convenient alternative to indoor CO_2-intensive pastimes such as watching TV and playing computer games. Secondly, in term of community, outdoor leisure activities can be promoted as a mean to promote community interaction and to a more pleasant and united community. Also, to better cultivate such a community, the citizens of the community should be included in the planning stage to co-create infrastructure. Finally, in terms of group activities, outdoor activities such as square dancing can be promoted as changes for socializing within the community.

Another key factor to affect residential CO_2 intensities is the sharing effect. The Chinese households are getting smaller with fewer children and the gradual disintegration of multi-generation cohabitation. For example, residential CO_2 emissions in rural lifestyles witnessed the greatest increase from 2008 to 2018. The number of family members shrank significantly by 38% in rural lifestyles and only 16% in urban lifestyles. More and more residential activities are individualized. For example, the importance of watching TV has been in relative decline in comparison to other leisure and socializing activities, especially with the much wider penetration of the Internet and availability of Internet-access devices such as computers, smart phones and tablets. Our suggestion here, to promote low CO_2 intensive outdoor activities as social activities in the community, might perhaps serve as a bridge within the community to strengthen cohesion and lead to sharing society to further reduce CO_2 emissions.

References

Anderson, B. (2016). Laundry, energy and time: Insights from 20 years of time-use diary data in the United Kingdom. *Energy Research & Social Science*, *22*, 125–136. doi: 10.1016/j.erss.2016.09.004

Ariely, D. (2008). *Predictably irrational: The hidden forces that shape our decisions*. New York, NY: Harper Audio.

Ariely, D. (2011). The upside of irrationality. *Paper presented at the 2011 Aerospace Conference*, MT, USA: Big Sky.

BP. (2021). *Statistical Review of World Energy*. Retrieved from: https://www.bp.com/en/global/corporate/energy-economics/statistical-review-of-world-energy.html

Byerly, H., Balmford, A., Ferraro, P. J., Hammond Wagner, C., Palchak, E., Polasky, S., … Fisher, B. (2018). Nudging pro-environmental behavior: Evidence and opportunities. *Frontiers in Ecology and the Environment*, *16*(3), 159–168. doi: 10.1002/fee.1777

Chen, C. F., Zarazua de Rubens, G., Xu, X., & Li, J. (2020). Coronavirus comes home? Energy use, home energy management, and the social-psychological factors of COVID-19. *Energy Research & Social Science*, *68*, 101688. doi: 10.1016/j.erss.2020.101688

Costa, D. L., & Kahn, M. E. (2013). Energy conservation "Nudges" and environmentalist ideology: Evidence from a randomized residential electricity field experiment. *Journal of the European Economic Association*, *11*(3), 680–702. doi: 10.1111/jeea.12011

Damgaard, M. T., & Nielsen, H. S. (2018). Nudging in education. *Economics of Education Review*, *64*, 313–342. doi:10.1016/j.econedurev.2018.03.008

Darby, S. (2010). Smart metering: What potential for householder engagement? *Building Research & Information*, *38*(5), 442–457. doi: 10.1080/09613218.2010.492660

DeBondt, W., Forbes, W., Hamalainen, P., & Gulnur Muradoglu, Y. (2010). What can behavioural finance teach us about finance? *Qualitative Research in Financial Markets*, *2*(1), 29–36. doi: 10.1108/17554171011042371

Delmas, M. A., Fischlein, M., & Asensio, O. I. (2013). Information strategies and energy conservation behavior: A meta-analysis of experimental studies from 1975 to 2012. *Energy Policy*, *61*, 729–739. doi: 10.1016/j.enpol.2013.05.109

Demarque, C., Charalambides, L., Hilton, D. J., & Waroquier, L. (2015). Nudging sustainable consumption: The use of descriptive norms to promote a minority behavior in a realistic online shopping environment. *Journal of Environmental Psychology*, *43*, 166–174. doi: 10.1016/j.jenvp.2015.06.008

Fischer, C. (2008). Feedback on household electricity consumption: A tool for saving energy? *Energy Efficiency, 1*(1), 79–104. doi: 10.1007/ s12053-008-9009-7

IPCC. (2006). *Guidelines for national greenhouse gas inventories* Retrieved from https://www.ipcc-nggip.iges.or.jp/public/2006gl/

IPCC. (2013). *Climate change 2013: The physical science basis*. Retrieved from

Kahneman, D. (2003). A perspective on judgment and choice: Mapping bounded rationality. *American Psychologist, 58*(9), 697–720. doi: 10.1037/0003-066X.58.9.697

Kahneman, D., & Tversky, A. (1979). On the interpretation of intuitive probability: A reply to Jonathan Cohen. *Cognition, 7*(4), 409–411. doi: 10.1016/0010-0277(79)90024-6

Krarti, M., & Aldubyan, M. (2021). Review analysis of COVID-19 impact on electricity demand for residential buildings. *Renewable and Sustainable Energy Reviews, 143*. doi: 10.1016/j.rser.2021.110888

Larsen, J. (2016). The making of a pro-cycling city: Social practices and bicycle mobilities. *Environment and Planning A: Economy and Space, 49*(4), 876–892. doi: 10.1177/0308518x16682732

National Bureau of Statistics. (2019). *China energy statistical yearbook*. Beijing, China: China Statistics Press.

Nicholls, L., & Strengers, Y. (2015). Peak demand and the 'family peak' period in Australia: Understanding practice (in)flexibility in households with children. *Energy Research & Social Science, 9*, 116–124. doi: 10.1016/j. erss.2015.08.018

Nielsen, A. S. E., Sand, H., Sørensen, P., Knutsson, M., Martinsson, P., Persson, E., & Wollbrant, C. (2017). *Nudging and pro-environmental behaviour*. Nordisk Ministerråd

Pucher, J., & Buehler, R. (2008). Making cycling irresistible: Lessons from The Netherlands, Denmark and Germany. *Transport Reviews, 28*(4), 495–528. doi: 10.1080/01441640701806612

Samuelson, W., & Zeckhauser, R. (1988). Status quo bias in decision making. *Journal of Risk and Uncertainty, 1*(1), 7–59. doi: 10.1007/bf00055564

Shove, E. (2003). *Comfort, cleanliness and convenience: The social organization of normality*. Oxford, UK: Berg.

Shove, E. (2010). Beyond the ABC: Climate change policy and theories of social change. *Environment and Planning A: Economy and Space, 42*(6), 1273–1285. doi: 10.1068/a42282

Shove, E., Pamtzar, M., & Watson, M. (2012). *The dynamics of social practice: Everyday life and how it changes*. London: SAGE Publications Ltd

Shove, E., Trentmann, F., & Wilk, R. (2009). *Time, consumption and everyday life: Practice, materiality and culture*. Oxford: Berg Publishers.

Shove, E., Walker, G., Tyfield, D., & Urry, J. (2014). What is energy for? social practice and energy demand. *Theory, Culture & Society, 31*(5), 41–58. doi: 10.1177/0263276414536746

Simon, H. A. (1972). Theories of bounded rationality. *Decision and Organization, 1*(1), 161–176.

Strengers, Y. (2012). Peak electricity demand and social practice theories: Reframing the role of change agents in the energy sector. *Energy Policy, 44,* 226–234. doi: 10.1016/j.enpol.2012.01.046

Strengers, Y., & Maller, C. (2011). Integrating health, housing and energy policies: Social practices of cooling. *Building Research & Information, 39*(2), 154–168. doi: 10.1080/09613218.2011.562720

Sullivan, O., Gershuny, J., Sevilla, A., Foliano, F., Vega-Rapun, M., Grignon, J. L., ... Walthery, P. (2021). Using time-use diaries to track changing behavior across successive stages of COVID-19 social restrictions. *Proceedings of the National Academy of Sciences of the United States of America, 118*(35). doi:10.1073/pnas.2101724118|1of7

Sunstein, C. R. (2014). Nudging: A very short guide. *Journal of Consumer Policy, 37*(4), 583–588. doi: 10.1007/s10603-014-9273-1

Thaler, R. H., & Sunstein, C. R. (2008). *Nudge: Improving decisions about health, wealth, and happiness.* New York, NY: Penguin Books.

Torriti, J., Hanna, R., Anderson, B., Yeboah, G., & Druckman, A. (2015). Peak residential electricity demand and social practices: Deriving flexibility and greenhouse gas intensities from time use and locational data. *Indoor and Built Environment, 24*(7), 891–912. doi: 10.1177/1420326x15600776

Vallgarda, S. (2012). Nudge: A new and better way to improve health? *Health Policy, 104*(2), 200–203. doi: 10.1016/j.healthpol.2011.10.013

Vandenbroele, J., Vermeir, I., Geuens, M., Slabbinck, H., & Van Kerckhove, A. (2020). Nudging to get our food choices on a sustainable track. *Proc Nutr Soc, 79*(1), 133–146. doi: 10.1017/S0029665119000971

WHO. (2021). *WHO Coronavirus (COVID-19) Dashboard.* Retrieved from https://covid19.who.int

Yao, X., & Zhang, Y. (2021). Understanding the changing household project and the pocket of local orders of home under the COVID-19: Case studies from residents of Shuangjing subdistrict in Beijing. *Urban Development Studies, 28,* 3–9.

Index

Pages followed by *italics* refer figures and **bold** refer tables and pages followed by n refer note.

absence (from residence) 72, **73**, 75, 76, *94*, *96*, *97*; activity categorization (comparisons) **101**; emissions (2008 to 2018) *111*; emissions by age *120–122*; emissions by educational status *123–125*; emissions by income level *125–127*; gendered emissions *117–119*; residential emissions (2018) *109*, *110*; rural emissions *113*, *114*; time spent on activities (2050 projection) *140*; time-use and CO_2 intensity effects *142*; urban emissions *112*, *114*; weekday versus weekend emissions *115*, *116*

active occupancy (concept) 70, 72

actively-occupied (occupancy status) 72, 75

activities: hours per day 76; residential carbon dioxide intensities 23; residential emissions 109–127; time-use diary **64**; time-use intensities 22

activity classification 33, **58–63**, **66**

activity location 58, **101**

activity-appliance matching **73**, 95

activity-related appliances (category) **74**, 75, 76, 87–95, 147, 153; activity categorization (comparisons) **102**; carbon dioxide intensity effect 141, *142*; emission

reductions (additional hour per day spent on outdoor activities) 144, *144*, *145*, 146; emissions (2008–2018) *111*; emissions (rural vs urban) 113, *114*; emissions (weekday versus weekend) *115*, *116*; expected usage behavior **104**; gendered lifestyle emissions *118*, *119*; residential emissions 109, *110*; share of emissions *110*; time-use effects *143*; variables **99**, **100**

additional hour per day on outdoor activities 143–146, 148

age 9, 22, 33, **34**, **35**, **57**, **80**; lifestyle evolution (2018 vs 2008) *49*; lifestyle variations *46*; residential emissions 119–122

age dependency ratio 133, *134*

aging population 21, 23, 131, 133, *134*, 148; climate impacts of demographic shifts 134, 137–139, *140*; relevance to energy consumption 13, 14

air conditioner 69, **73**, 75, 83, *84*, *87*, *89*, 90, *92*, *93*, **104**, 115; power rates *85*; variables **98**, **99**

American Time-Use Survey (ATUS) 16, 31, 37

Anhui province 31, *32*, *78*, **81**

appliance characteristics 37, 86–91; mending mismatched datasets 83, *84*, *85*

appliance ownership 83, 86, 87, 90; urban vs rural households *87*, 87

appliance power rate 87, 88, 91

appliance variables **98–100**

appliances 8, 14, 69, 131; daily usage 88–90; energy-intensive 12; hours per day in operation 76; number of household members involved in an activity 91, 92, *92*; occupancy groups **104**; operation modes **73, 74**, *142*; power rating 76; time-saving versus non-time-saving **99, 100**; time-use characteristics 18

Asia 10

background appliances (category) **73**, 75, 87–93, *94*, *96*, *97*, **104**, 147; carbon dioxide intensity effect 141, *142*; change of emissions (2008–2018) *111*; emission reductions (additional hour per day spent on outdoor activities) 144, *144*, *145*; emissions (rural vs urban, 2008–2018) *114*, 115; gendered lifestyle emissions *118*, *119*; residential emissions 109, *110*; share of emissions *110*; time-use effects *143*; variables **98**; weekday versus weekend emissions *115*, *116*

baseline emission factors (China) 77

Basner, M. 16

behavioral economics 150, 151

behavioral energy studies 37

Beijing province 11, 31, *32*, *78*, **81**

Bevans 15

bicycles 152, 153

Bin, S. 7

bottom-up approach 7, 22, 147; residential electricity demand models 18, 19

bottom-up approach for constructing electricity intensity 72–76; activity-appliance matching **73**, **74**; electricity intensity 75, 76; matching electric appliances with activities 72–75; theorem (Equation 3.1) 76

bread machine **74**, *87–89*, *92*, *93*; variables **99**

Buehler, R. 152

Bush, George H. W. xiv

Capsso, A. 18, 70

carbon dioxide (CO_2) emissions xiii, xiv, 1, 12, 22; by activity (Equation 4.1) 108; associated with residential electricity consumption 21; daily (Equation 4.2) 108; per hour per person 68, 75, 76; residential 23, 108–130

carbon dioxide intensity (emissions per unit of GDP) xiii, 1, 20–23, 109, 129, 130; direct versus indirect 69

carbon dioxide intensity of activities 76, 95–97, 131, 134, 144, 147, 148; definition 141; estimation methods 69

carbon dioxide intensity of time-use activity 22, 68–107

carbon mitigation: time-use management 23, 147–156

carbon neutrality xiii, 2, 4

caring activities **61**, **62**

Catrine, T. L. 16

Chen, B. 9

child care **36**, **64**, **66**

China: carbon emissions 2, 3; carbon emissions per capita (1990–2020) 1, *2*; carbon neutrality target date (2060) 3, 4, 153; demographic shifts 131–134; fuel mix (1980–2019) *4*; GDP growth xiii; largest emitting country in world 1, 9, 10; peak emissions target date (2030) 3, 4, 153; population 3; population projections 134; primary energy consumption (1980–2019) *3*, *4*; residential sector 1–7; statistical yearbooks 79, 82, 85, 86, 93, 95; time use 22, 31–66; urbanization versus energy use (regional differences) 11; urbanization rate (1980–2019) 10

China Energy Label standards 79, 82, 84

Chinese emissions factor 95–97

Chinese Family Panel Studies 82
Chinese Household Survey 31, 32
Chinese Residential Energy
  Consumption Survey (CRECS,
  2012) xiv, 77–79, *78*, **80**, **81**, 86, 87,
  88, 95, **100n1**; appliance variables
  98–100; criteria 78; data quality
  78; household characteristics **81**;
  mending mismatched datasets
  82–86; population distribution
  81; profile of samples 79;
  questionnaire 79; sampled
  provinces *78*; variables **80**
climate change: China's residential
  sector 1–7
climate impacts 23, 131–146;
  demographic shifts 134–137, *135–
  140*; 139; time-use management
  143–146; time-use patterns 141–143
climate-friendly time-use patterns
  150–154
coal *3*, *4*, 12, 148, *149*; residential
  consumption (1980–2019) 5, *6*
commuting 14, 16, 20
computers 15, **74**, 75, 83, *84*, *87–89*,
  92, *93*, **104**, 154; variables **100**
consumer lifestyle approach
  (CLA) 7
cooker **74**, *87*, *89*, 90, *92*, *93*, 94, **104**;
  variables **99**
cooking 10; fuel and devices 8; most
  energy-consuming activity 70
Copenhagen 152, 153
Copenhagen Accord 1, *2*
COVID-19 pandemic xiv, 3, 150
CTUS (Chinese Time-Use Survey)
  xiv, 17, 31–35, **36**, 37, 77, 108;
  mending mismatched datasets
  82–86
CTUS (2008) 32–35, 91, 93,
  147; activity categories
  (harmonization) 35, **36**; activity
  categorization **101–103**;
  demographic statistics 33, **34**, **35**;
  gendered lifestyles 43–46; life stage
  and lifestyles 46–49; urban and
  rural lifestyles 39–43
CTUS (2018) 32, 33, 35, 91, 92, 147;
  activity categorization **101–103**;
  demographic statistics 33, **34**;

lifestyle (typical weekday) *37*,
  39; lifestyle (typical weekend or
  holiday) *38–39*; lifestyle evolution
  (since 2008) *39*; time-use diary **64**
cross-country studies: urbanization
  versus energy consumption 11

daily usage (variable) 83, 86
data collection 33, 77, 78
data deficiencies 68, 70, 76, 91–93,
  95, 108, 129
datasets 21; failure to match 21
datasets (mending mismatches) 82–
  86; appliance characteristics 83,
  84, *85*; household demographic
  characteristics 85, 86; time-use
  patterns 82, *83*
day reconstruction method 16–17
decomposition analysis 19, 20,
  131; climate impacts of time-use
  patterns 143
demand-side management 18, 68
demographic change 12–14, 23,
  131–146, 148; climate impacts
  134–137, *135–140*, 139
demographic profiles 23
demographic statistics 33, **34**
Denmark 18, 152
developed countries 4, 10, 21, 77,
  129, 133
developing countries 13, 21, 77;
  energy consumption (rural-urban
  contrast) 10
diary episode files 34, 35, **35**
Ding, Q. 8
Donglan, Z. 12
Dowlatabadi, H. 7
Druckman, A. 20
duration of use **98–100**
dwelling characteristics 13, 79, **80**
dwelling size (variable) 79, **80**, **81**;
  rural versus urban 85, *86*

Earth Summit (Rio de Janeiro, 1992)
  xiii, xiv
economic development 3, 7, 12,
  133, 147
economic growth 4, 129
economic reform era 5, 50, 129,
  130, 132

educational level 22, 33, **34**, **35**, **80**, 147
educational level (lifestyles) 49–52; residential emissions 122–124, *125*, 128, 129
elderly population **64**, **66**, 131, 137; "old people" 22; "seniors" 152
electric appliances 18, 22, 130; characteristics 147; electricity intensity 79; emissions 109; matched with activities 72–75; occupancy groups 79
electric heater **73**, 75, *87–89*, *92*, *93*, **104**, 115; variables **98**
electric stove **74**, 75, *87–89*, 90, *92*, *93*, **104**; variables **99**
electricity *3*, *4*, 7, 10, 12, 18, 148, *149*; carbon dioxide emission factor 75; household demand 70; load profiles 70
electricity billing 79, **80**
electricity consumption *6*, 22, 55, 71, 90, 91; residential emissions (projected age profiles, 2010–2050) *138*, *139*
electricity demand 70, **71**
electricity intensity 75, 76, 109
electricity intensity of activities 70, 79, 91; estimation methods 69
Elliott, R. J. R. 11
empirical studies 21, 75, 153
employment 14, **36**, **59**, **64**, **66**
energy: expenditure 7; necessity in daily life 68; pricing 12
energy consumption 7; direct and indirect 7, 8, 20; rural-urban contrast 10; time use and 17–21
energy efficiency 7, 11, 68, **80**, 84, 87, 88, 90
energy intensity 19–21
energy intensity of time use: estimation 68–72
Energy Label Standards *85*, 86, **98–100**
Energy Statistical Yearbook 93
energy use 151; social and behavioral perspectives 7
energy-use bill data 69, **71**
Environmental Kuznets Curve 133
estimating residential electricity 22, 68–107; activity

categorization (comparison) **101–103**; appliance characteristics (2008, 2018) 86–91; appliance occupancy groups **104**; appliance variables **98–100**; changes (2008–2018) 86–97; mending mismatched datasets 82–86; reconstructed intensity of activity (2008, 2018) 93–97; sharing characteristics 91–93
estimating residential electricity (data) 77–86; CRECS 77–79, *78*, **80**, **81**; mending mismatched datasets 82–86
Europe 133
European Union 1; carbon emissions (1990–2020) *2*
Eurostat 15, 77
everyday activities 14, 19–21, 69, 70, 72, 147; ecological impact **71**

family 131, 137
family division of labor 52
family members **57**
family size 153
family studies literature: gendered division of labor 14
fan **73**, *87–89*, *92*, *93*, **104**; variables **99**
fertility rate (sub-replacement) 13
Finland 19, 20; direct intensity of activities 69; two-person households 69
first tier activities **66**
Fischer, D. 18
floor heating *87–89*, *92*, *93*, **104**; variables **98**
food 7, 19, **60**, **74**, 151
formal employment **64**, **66**
fossil fuels 1, 68, 133
free time **66**
freezer **73**, 75, *87–89*, *92*, *93*, **104**; power rates 84, *85*; variables **98**
friends **57**, **65**

games **63**
Gansu province 31, *32*, *78*, **81**
GDP xiii, 12; inclusion of unpaid housework 16

gender 9, 16, 22, 33, **34**, **35**, **80**, 127–129; factor affecting residential energy consumption 13
gendered lifestyles 43–46, 147; differences and evolution (2008–2018) *44*; residential emissions 116–119; weekends and holidays (2008–2018) *45*
generation gap 129
geographic context 17
Germany 5, 18, 148, 152
globalization 9, 10
GPS devices 78
Greece 144, 148
greenhouse gases (GHGs) 1, 9, 23, 128
Guangdong province 31, *32*, *78*, 79, **81**
Guerra Santin, O. 8

Harmonized Activity Classification for Time-Use Surveys in Europe 16
Harmonized European Time-Use Surveys 31, 37
heating 8, 148, *149*
Hebei province 31, *32*, *78*, **81**
Heilongjiang province 31, *32*, *78*, **81**
Heinonen, J. 20
Henan province 31, *32*, *78*, **81**
high school 47
high-income countries 11
high-income lifestyle 52, *54*
hobbies **63**
Hokao, K. 8
holiday lifestyle 37–39, 41, 128; residential emissions *115*, *116*
holidays: effect of pandemic 150; in-residence versus absence from residence 55
homework (educational) **62**
Hong Kong 17
household appliances 69, 70, 79, **80**; power characteristics **71**; temporal characteristics of power consumption 71
household characteristics 37, 79, **81**
household chores 38, 116, 128, 129, 130, 148

household demographics 79, **80**; mending mismatched datasets 85, 86
household expenditure survey 19, 69, **71**
household head 33, 77
household income 12, **81**; rural versus urban 85, *86*
household information 32, 33
household members **65**; number involved in activity matched to appliance 91, 92, *92*; time spent on activities matched to an appliance 92, 93
household primary production **59**
household production **64**, **66**
household secondary production and construction **59**, **60**
household service production **60**
household size 21, 76, 79, **80**, **81**; predictor of residential energy use 13; rural versus urban 85, *86*
household types 19, 20
housewives 15, 52
housework 15, 16, 22, **64**, **66**, 117
housing 7, 20
hukou system 112
HVAC appliances 88, **104**, 150

in-residence activities **73**, 75
in-residence hours **73**
income 7, 12, 22, 33, **34**, **35**, 79, **80**, 147
income levels (lifestyles): emissions 124–127, 128, 129
income and lifestyles (2008–2018) 52–54
index decomposition analysis (IDA) 8
India *2*, 5
industrial upgrading: urbanization (direct and indirect effects) 11
industrialization 4, 9
input-output 8, 19, 69, **71**
Institute of Social Science Survey (ISSS, Peking University) 82, *83*
interdisciplinary research 21
Intergovernmental Panel on Climate Change (IPCC) 1

Interim National Energy
   Consumption Survey (USA) 77
International Association for
   Time-Use Research (IATUR) 15
International Classification of
   Activities for Time-Use Statistics 15
International Energy Agency
   77, 95, 97
International Time-Use Survey 31
Internet 38, 49, 50, **62**, **65**, **74**,
   119, 153
IPAT model 8

Jalas, M. 19, 20, 69
Japan *2*, 5
Ji, X. 9
Juntunen, J. K. 20, 69

Kahneman, D. 17
Kaneko, S. 9, 11
Kosovo 77
Kyoto Protocol (1997) 1, *2*

Landefeld, J. S. 16
Larsen, J. 152
leisure and socializing **36**, 37–39, *40*,
   41, *42*, 43, *43–45*, 46, 47, *48*, 49,
   50–56, 52, **62–64**, **66**, **74**, *94*, *96*,
   97, 153; activity categorization
   (comparisons) **103**; emission
   reductions (additional hour per
   day spent on outdoor activities)
   145; emissions (2008 to 2018)
   111; emissions by age 119,
   120–122, 128, 137; emissions
   by educational status *123–125*;
   emissions by income level
   125–127; gendered emissions
   117–119, 128; general time-use
   pattern (2008, 2012, 2018) 82,
   83; residential emissions (2018)
   109, *110*; rural emissions *113*,
   114; time spent on activities (2050
   projection) *140*; time-use and CO_2
   intensity effects *142*; time-use
   effect 141; urban emissions *112*,
   114; weekday versus weekend
   emissions *115*, *116*
leisure time 16
life stage and lifestyles 46–49

lifestyle: education and 49–52;
   income and (2008–2018) 52–54;
   life stage and 46–49; residential
   energy consumption 7–14; typical
   weekday (2018) *37*; typical
   weekend or holiday (2018) *38*;
   urban versus rural 39–43
lifestyle factors: everyday activities
   (patterns and locations) 9
lifestyles 21, 22, 148; climate impacts
   23, 131–146; residential emissions
   23, 108–130
light **73**, *87–89*, 90, *92*, *93*, **104**;
   variables **99**
Lin, B. 9
load curve 37, 70
load profiles 150
low-income countries 11
low-income lifestyle 52, *53*, 54

marital status 17, **35**
Marszal-Pomianowska, A. 18
McCulla, S. H. 16
meals **36**, *37*, *38*, *40*, *44*, *47*, *48*,
   51, *53*, *54*, *56*, **58**, 69, 75, *94*,
   96, *97*; activity categorization
   (comparisons) **102**; emission
   reductions (additional hour per
   day spent on outdoor activities)
   145; emissions (2008 to 2018)
   111; emissions by age *120–122*;
   emissions by educational status
   123–125; emissions by income
   level *125–127*; gendered emissions
   117–119; residential emissions
   (2018) *109*, *110*; rural emissions
   113, *114*; time spent on activities
   (2050 projection) *140*; time-
   use and CO_2 intensity effects
   142; urban emissions *112*,
   114; weekday versus weekend
   emissions *115*, *116*
men 116; emissions 116–119;
   emissions (gender inequalities)
   127, 128; typical lifestyle (2018) *44*
Michelson, W. H. 16
micro-level approach 36
microdata xiv, 34
microwave oven *84*, *87–89*, 90, *92*,
   93, **104**, 117; variables **99**

middle-income countries 11
mortality rate 13
Moscow 15
Multinational Time-Use Study 15

National Bureau of Statistics (NBS) xiv, 31, 34, 79, **81**, *96*
national statistics 93, 95
natural gas *3, 4*, 10, 12, 148, *149*; residential consumption (1980–2019) *6*
natural and social temporal rhythms 70, 71
Netherlands 152
New-Type Urbanization Plan 11
no-schooling (people with): daily emissions *123–125*; typical lifestyle (2018) 49, 50, *51*
non-SNA productive activities **66**
Norway 143, 144, 148
nudge (behavioral economics) 150, 151
numeric codes (standardized) 33

occupancy status 72, 75, 76
occupancy-related appliances (category) **73**, 75, 87–93, *94, 96, 97*, 147, 153; activity categorization (comparisons) **102**; carbon dioxide intensity effect 141, *142*; change of emissions (2008–2018) *111*; emission reductions (additional hour per day spent on outdoor activities) 144, *144, 145*, 146; emissions (rural vs urban, 2008–2018) 113, *114*; expected usage behavior **104**; gendered lifestyle emissions *118, 119*; residential emissions 109, *110*; share of emissions *110*; time-use effects *143*; variables **98, 99**; weekday versus weekend emissions *115, 116*
office equipment **74**, 75, 87–89, *92, 93*
oil *3, 4*, 12, 148, *149*, 150; residential consumption (1980–2019) *6*
online market information 79, **98–100**
Organization for Economic Co-operation and Development

(OECD) 3; carbon emissions (1990–2020) *2*
outdoor activities 23, 153; additional hour per day 143–146; effect of pandemic 150
"Outline for Development of Chinese Women (2001–2010)" 31
Ouyang, J. 8
oven **74**, *87–89, 92, 93*, **104**; variables **99**

paid work 36, 37, *37–56*, **74**, *94, 96, 97*; activity categorization (comparisons) **101**; emission reductions (additional hour per day spent on outdoor activities) *145*; emissions (2008 to 2018) *111*; emissions by age *120–122*; emissions by educational status *123–125*; emissions by income level *125–127*; gendered emissions *117–119*; general time-use pattern (2008, 2012, 2018) *83*; residential emissions (2018) *109, 110*; rural emissions *113, 114*; time spent on activities (2050 projection) *140*; time-use and CO_2 intensity effects *142*; urban emissions *112, 114*; weekday versus weekend emissions *115, 116*
Paris Agreement xiii, 1, *2*
passively-occupied (occupancy status) 72, 75
personal care and maintenance 36, *37, 38, 40, 43, 44, 48, 51, 53, 54, 56*, **58, 59**, *74, 94, 96, 97*; activity categorization (comparisons) **101**; carbon dioxide intensity effect 141; emission reductions (additional hour per day spent on outdoor activities) *145*, 146; emissions (2008 to 2018) *111*; emissions by age *120–122*; emissions by educational status *123–125*; emissions by income level *125–127*; gendered emissions *117–119*; general time-use pattern (2008, 2012, 2018) *83*; high electricity and CO_2 intensities 147; residential emissions (2018)

109, *110*; rural emissions *113*, *114*; time spent on activities (2050 projection) *140*; time-use and CO$_2$ intensity effects *142*; time-use effect 141; urban emissions *112*, *114*; weekday versus weekend emissions *115*, *116*

personal hygiene **58**, **59**, **64**, **66**; *see also* showering

personal information file 34, 35, **35**

physical activity 16

physical environment 17, 152

population: age groups (1950–2050) *138*

population growth 10, 19

post-diary questions 32, 33

Poumanyvong, P. 9, 11

power consumption characteristics 69, 70

power rate (variable) **80**, 83, 84, 86, **98–100**

practical knowledge 152

pressure cooker **74**, *87–89*, 90, *92*, *93*; variables **99**

primary activity 32, 33

primary schooling *50*

primary sector: energy consumption (1995–2019) 4, *5*

private vehicles 13, 39, 79, **80**, 148, 152

provinces 33, **34**, **35**, **81**

Pucher, J. 152

purchasing goods and services **61**

quality of life 16

quantitative studies 14, 23

questionnaires 32

Radcliffe College: Murray Centre 15

radiator **73**, *87–89*, *92*, *93*, **104**; variables **98**

Ramírez-Mendiola, J. L. 18

reading **62**, **64**, **66**

reconstructed electricity intensity of activity (2008, 2018) 93–97; before calibration with national statistics 93–95; calibration by residential consumption (daily, per capita) 95, *96*; carbon dioxide intensity of activity 95–97

refrigerator 69, **73**, 75, 83, *84*, *87–89*, 90, *92*, *93*, **104**, 150; power rates 84, *85*; variables **98**

Renmin University xiv, 78

residential carbon dioxide emissions 22, 23, 141; by activities 109–127; by activity and operation mode of appliances (2018) *110*; by fuel (2008, 2018) *149*; lifestyles 22, 108–130; reconstructing 108; time use and 147–150

residential electricity consumption 21, 108; daily 93, 95, *96*; direct **71**

residential electricity demand: intra-day fluctuations 71, 72

residential electricity intensity of activities 147

residential energy consumption 70; two causes affecting 72

residential energy consumption factors: demographic change 12–14; lifestyle 7–9; urbanization 9–12

residential sector: energy consumption (1995–2019) 4, 5, *5*, *6*

residential survey data 22

residential unit: definition 77

retail stores (opening hours) 9

retirement lifestyle 119, *121*, *122*, 128, 139, 148; evolution (2018 vs 2008) *49*; typical lifestyle (2018) 47, *48*

rice cookers 117

Richardson, I. 18, 70, 71, 72

roads 39

rural areas 15, **80**, 108

rural households 79, **81**; appliance characteristics 86–91; appliance ownership 83, *84*; appliance use (sharing characteristics) 91–93; average size 91; carbon dioxide intensity of activity 95–97; electricity consumption 90, 91, 95, *96*

rural lifestyle 22, 39–43, 147, 153; emissions (2008–2018) *114*; differences and evolution (2008–2018) *42*; residential emissions 112–115, 129

rural residential sector 12

rural residents 8, 33, **34**, **35**, 76, 141; energy intensity of activity before calibration 93–95; residential carbon dioxide intensities 23
Russia 5

sample size 31, 70, 95
scale effect xiii
Schipper, L. 9, 17
Schwanen, T. 17
second tier activities **66**
secondary activity 32, 33
secondary sector: energy consumption (1995–2019) 4, *5*
sensitivity analysis 131, 132, 143
service sector employment 16
Shahbaz, M. 9
Shandong province *78*, *79*, **81**
Shanghai 11
Shanghai province *78*, **81**
sharing 147, 153
showering and bathing 19, **58**, 71, **74**, 75, **101**; *see also* personal hygiene
Sichuan province 21, 31, *32*, 33, *78*, **81**
sleep 16, **36**, *37–39*, *43*, *44*, *47*, *48*, *51*, *53*, *54*, *56*, **58**, **64**, **66**, **73**, *94*, *96*, *97*, 143; carbon dioxide intensity effect 141; emissions (2008 to 2018) *111*; emissions by age *120–122*; emissions by educational status *123–125*; emissions by income level *125–127*; gendered emissions *117–119*; general time-use pattern (2008, 2012, 2018) *83*; residential emissions (2018) *109*, *110*; rural emissions *113*, *114*; time spent on activities (2050 projection) *140*; time-use and CO_2 intensity effects *142*; urban emissions *112*, *114*; weekday versus weekend emissions *115*, *116*
smart phones 38, 79, 154
social practice theories 151, 152
social practices (constraints imposed by) 9
social rhythm 115
socialization: gender roles 13
socio-economic features 35, 147

Soviet Union 15
space heating 10, 69, 79, **80**
spatial lifestyles: in-residence versus absence from residence 54–55, *56*
sports **63**
square dancing 153
statistical categories: failure to match 21
statistics 15, 22, 77–79, 129
Statistics Sweden 31
STIRPAT model 8, 9
Stone, Philip 15
strangers **57**, **65**
study **36**, *37*, *38*, *40*, *43*, *44*, *47–56*, **62**, **64**, **66**, **74**, *94*, *96*, *97*; activity categorization (comparisons) **102**; emission reductions (additional hour per day spent on outdoor activities) *145*; emissions (2008 to 2018) *111*; emissions by age 119, *120–122*; emissions by educational status *123–125*; emissions by income level *125–127*; gendered emissions *117–119*; general time-use pattern (2008, 2012, 2018) *83*; residential emissions (2018) *109*, *110*; rural emissions *113*, *114*; time spent on activities (2050 projection) *140*; time-use and CO_2 intensity effects *142*; urban emissions *112*, *114*; weekday versus weekend emissions *115*, *116*
Sweden 69, 144, 148
Switzerland 143, 144, 148

tech industry: infamous "996" work 41
technological advances 8, 15
television **74**, 75, 83, *84*, *87–89*, *92*, *93*, **104**; variables **100**; *see also* watching television
tertiary sector: energy consumption (1995–2019) 4, *5*
Texas 150
Thailand 77
third-tier activity categorization system 34
three-state model 72
time: incorporation in modeling energy demand 9

time use 14; on activities (effect of
pandemic) 150; China 22, 31–66;
and energy consumption 17–21;
linkage with energy consumption
xiv; residential lifestyle indicator
14–21
time-saving innovations: rebound
effects 9, 69
time-use activity 148; carbon dioxide
intensity 22, 23, 68–107
time-use data **71**, 72
time-use defined lifestyles 35–39,
37–40, 41, *41–43*, 43, *44–46*,
46, 47, *47–51*, 49, 50, 52, *52*,
53–55, 54, 55, *56*
time-use diary 32, 33, **57**; precoded
33; full-time post-coded 33
time-use effect: differences in
emissions (2008, 2018) *143*;
variations in emissions 141
time-use management: for carbon
mitigation 23, 147–156; climate
impacts 143–146
time-use measures 131, 132
time-use patterns 21–23, 32, 108,
109, 129, 131, 147, 148; climate
impacts 141–143; climate-friendly
150–154; mending mismatched
datasets 82, *83*
time-use perspective 134; residential
emissions 147–150
time-use perspective energy
consumption studies 68
time-use rebound effect 19
time-use studies 36, 37
time-use surveys 70; applications
14–17; data 22, 23, 69; sample
sizes 15
time-use variables 70
Torriti, J. 18, 19
transport 7, 22, 32, 58, **64**; modal
shift 152, 153
transportation 13, 14, **36**, 37–39, *40*,
41, *42*, 43, *43–45*, 46, 47, *48*, 49,
50–56, 52, **66**, 68, 150, 151; car
ownership 39; private use 79, **80**;
urbanization (direct and indirect
effects) 11
travel 8; effect of pandemic 150
two-person households 19

United Kingdom 15, 19, 20, 69;
time-use data 18
United Nations 15, 16, 23; UN
Department of Economic and
Social Affairs 14; UN Framework
Convention on Climate Change
(UNFCCC, 1992) xiii, 1; UN
World Population Prospects 134;
UNFPA 11
United States 1, 5, 7, 15, 17, 69,
129; carbon emissions (1990–
2020) 2; way of life "not up for
negotiations" (Bush Sr.) xiv
university education (people with) 47,
49, *50*, *51*; daily emissions *123–125*
unpaid domestic work **60–62**
unpaid work **36**, 37–39, *40*, 41, *42*,
43, *43–45*, 46, 47, *48*, 49, *50–56*,
52, **74**, *94*, *96*, *97*, 144; activity
categorization (comparisons)
102; carbon dioxide intensity
141; effect of pandemic 150;
emission reductions (additional
hour per day spent on outdoor
activities) *145*; emissions (2008
to 2018) *111*; emissions by age
119, *120–122*, 128; emissions by
educational status 122, *123–125*;
emissions by income level *125–
127*; gendered emissions *117–119*,
128; general time-use pattern
(2008, 2012, 2018) *83*; high
electricity and CO_2 intensities
147; most important component
in emissions 127; residential
emissions (2018) *109*, *110*;
residential CO_2 emissions (crucial
role) 148; rural emissions *113*,
114; time spent on activities (2050
projection) *140*; time-use and CO_2
intensity effects *142*; time-use
effect 141; urban emissions *112*,
114; weekday versus weekend
emissions *115*, *116*
urban areas **80**, 108;
disproportionate carbon emissions
10; parks 153; proportion of total
population 132, *132*
urban environment transition
theory 11

urban households 8, **81**; appliance characteristics 86–91; appliance ownership 83, 84, *84*; appliance use (sharing characteristics) 91–93; average size 91; carbon dioxide intensity of activity 95–97; electricity consumption 90, 91; electricity consumption (daily, per capita) 95, *96*

urban lifestyle 22, 39–43, 147, 153; differences and evolution (2008–2018) *42*; emissions (2008–2018) *114*; residential emissions 112–115, 129

urban planning 23, 153

urban residents 8, 12, 33, **34**, **35**, 76, 79, 141; energy intensity of activity before calibration 93–95; residential carbon dioxide intensities 23; time-use pattern (2008–2018) 82

urbanization 7, 9–12, 23, 112, 131, 148; agglomeration effect 133; climate impacts of demographic shifts 134, 135, 136, *137*; direct and indirect effects for energy use 12; ecological impacts 69; impacts on energy consumption 10, 11; links with energy use 10

urbanization rate 10, *132*, 132, 133

US Energy Information Administration 77

US Residential Energy Consumption Survey 79

usage frequency **98–100**

Wäckelgård, E. 18, 70, 71, 75, 76

Wang, C. 9

Wang, D. 17

Wang, P. 9

Wang, Q. 11

washing machines 71, **74**, 83, *84*, *87–89*, 90, *92*, *93*, **104**, 147; variables **99**

watching television **36**, 37–39, *40*, 41, *42*, 43, *43–45*, 46, 47, *48*, 49, *50–56*, 52, **62**, **64**, **66**, 69, 71, **74**, 75, *94*, *96*, *97*, 153; activity categorization (comparisons)

103; carbon dioxide intensity effect 141; emission reductions (additional hour per day spent on outdoor activities) *145*, 146; emissions (2008 to 2018) *111*; emissions by age 119, *120–122*, 128, 137; emissions by educational status *123–125*; emissions by income level *125–127*; gendered emissions *117–119*, 128; general time-use pattern (2008, 2012, 2018) 82, *83*; high electricity and CO_2 intensities 147; residential emissions (2018) *109*, *110*; rural emissions *113*, *114*; time spent on activities (2050 projection) *140*; time-use and CO_2 intensity effects *142*; time-use effect 141; urban emissions *112*, *114*; weekday versus weekend emissions *115*, *116*

water heater 10, **74**, 75, *84*, *87–89*, *92*, *93*, 94, **104**, 147; variables **99**, **100**

wealth versus personal happiness 17

weekday lifestyle 37–39, 128, 147; emissions *115*, *116*; urban versus rural *41*

weekdays 22, 32, **34**, **35**; effect of pandemic 150; general time-use pattern (2008, 2012, 2018) *83*; in-residence versus absence from residence 55, *56*

weekend 22, 32, **34**, **35**; effect of pandemic 150; general time-use pattern (2008, 2012, 2018) *83*; in-residence versus absence from residence 55, *56*

weekend lifestyle 37–39, 41, 128; emissions *115*, *116*; urban versus rural (2008–2018) *41*

Wei, Y. M. 7, 8

Widén, J. 18, 70, 71, 75, 76

Wiedenhofer, D. 20

women 22, 152; emissions 116–119; emissions (gender inequalities) 127–129; lifestyle 148; pro-environmental attitudes 14; rural activities 15; rural, elderly 70; typical lifestyle by daily time use (2018) *43*

Wong, Pui Ki xiv
working age people 13; lifestyle 119,
    120–122, 128; lifestyle evolution
    (2018 vs 2008) *49*; typical lifestyle
    (2018) 47, *48*
Working Group on Time Budgets
    and Social Activities (1970–) 15

Xu, B. 9
Xu, Y. 20
Xu, Yuan xiii, xiv

youth lifestyle 119, *120–122*, 128;
    evolution (2018 vs 2008) *49*;
    typical *47*
Yu, B. 20–21, 70
Yunnan province 31, *32*, *78*, **81**

Zhao, X. 12
Zhejiang province 31, *32*,
    78, **81**
Zheng, X. 10
Zhou, H. 17

For Product Safety Concerns and Information please contact our EU
representative GPSR@taylorandfrancis.com Taylor & Francis Verlag GmbH,
Kaufingerstraße 24, 80331 München, Germany

Printed and bound by CPI Group (UK) Ltd, Croydon, CR0 4YY

11/04/2025

01844010-0019